British Protestant Missions

British Protestant Missions

A. J. Temu, PhD
Department of History, University of Dar es Salaam

Longman

Longman Group Limited
London

*Associated companies, branches and representatives
throughout the world*

© Longman Group Limited 1972

First published 1972

ISBN 0 582 64559 X (Cased)
ISBN 0 582 64560 3 (Paper)

Printed in Great Britain
By Willmer Brothers Limited
Birkenhead

Contents

Preface   *page* 1

Introduction   5

1 The Freed Slave Settlement and Relations with the Arabs,
   1874–1890   11

2 Missionary Work and Expansion, 1874–1892   32

3 The Changing Situation and the Abolition of Slavery,
   1890–1907   43

4 The Liberated Africans on the Mombasa Coast, 1874-1904   63

5 Missionary Expansion, the Acquisition of Land and the
   Disruption of African Society, 1900–1914   91

6 Missionary Attitudes and Actions Towards Forced Labour,
   Native Paramountcy and African Politics, 1919–1925   117

7 The Parting of the Ways, 1875–1929   140

Bibliography   169

Index   181

Maps

1 Location Sketch: African catechists in areas and villages around the Kenya coast 67

2 Sketch map showing British Mission stations in Kenya east of the rift valley 99

Plates

Between pages 56–57

1 Freretown Mission School, 1875

2 Slaves in Chains

Between pages 88–89

3 Reverend W. S. Price

4 Slave's Deed of Freedom

5 Boys' School, Freretown

Acknowledgement

The publishers are grateful to the Church Missionary Society for permission to reproduce the illustrations in this book.

For my parents

Preface

This study has grown out of my doctoral thesis presented to the University of Alberta, Edmonton, in the spring of 1967. Professor Roland Oliver's pioneering work on the missionary factor in East Africa inspired me into undertaking this study. But more specific inspiration and encouragement were given me by Professor Donald L. Wiedner, then at the University of Alberta, now at Temple University, who supervised my thesis. I am deeply indebted to him for his good guidance, comments and criticisms, all of which made the thesis what it finally became. I am also grateful to my internal examiners, Professors H. A. Honcioski, Joseph G. Rayback, Brian Heeney and to my external examiner Professor Donald C. Savage, who so generously suggested many improvements.

This study in many ways follows in the footsteps of that of Professors A. F. A. Ajayi and E. A. Ayendele who, drawing inspiration from Professor Oliver's work, also made a study of the missions in Nigeria and explored different aspects of their work in their country which led to a new interpretation of the missionary work in that region. Theirs was in many ways a departure from many of the hitherto published literature on the missions, many of which had been published by the missionaries themselves. While laying no claim to have explored this subject for Kenya with the thoroughness, lucidity and vigour of my Western African colleagues, I have attempted, albeit in a modest way, to recast the work of the missions in this area from an African viewpoint, and I have explored some aspects of their work in the light of the new outlook now current in African history. To this extent, it is a *reinterpretation*.

I

Certainly the role of the missions in Kenya is of special interest, particularly when the colonial history of that country in which the missionaries feature so prominently ended with a violent confrontation between the Africans and their colonisers comparable with the violence which erupted in Algeria in 1954–1961. In Kenya, this violence, the Mau Mau war, broke out in 1952 and ended in 1956. Both these wars led to same sort of situation in the two countries: the dismantling of direct French rule in Algeria in 1961 and of British direct rule in Kenya in 1963. But the violence in Kenya was as much directed against the missions as it was against the British colonial administration. That is why a study of the work and role of the missions, here the British Protestant missions, bears special significance to the historian and to the public, as the missionaries have been tarred with the same brush as the colonial settler administration. This is vividly expressed in the Agikuyu saying *Gutiri muthungu na mubea* (there is no difference between the missionary and the white coloniser). Indeed we owe it to the new nation to reinterpret the role of the missions.

This study is necessarily confined to the early period during which the roots of the confrontation began to develop. The gap between the ruled and the rulers grew so wide in the first quarter of the twentieth century that the revolution seemed inevitable. Eruptions between the two sides occurred during that period and were suppressed, only to be postponed till 1952. So the story ends with 1929 when there was conflict between the Africans and the missions over cultural nationalism. For the period between 1929 and 1952 we must await another study.

Most of the chapters in this book focus therefore on the first twenty-nine or so years of the twentieth century of the colonial period which began in the latter part of the nineteenth century. In order to bring the work of the missions into proper perspective, I have inevitably gone back to the nineteenth century, in particular to the last twenty-seven years of that century when missionary work in Kenya began in earnest on the coast.

Many people helped me in the preparation of this monograph in one way or another. Certainly, it will be impossible to enumerate them all and I should like to record my appreciation of their help generally. I must, however, single out a few of these and pay special thanks to them. First, I am grateful to the students of the

University of Dar es Salaam to whom it has been my great pleasure and privilege to teach history for the last five years. All of them have helped to make me focus my study more sharply through the numerous questions that they raised in seminars and lectures. Secondly I should like to thank Professors T. O. Ranger and I. N. Kimambo who as Heads of the Department of History allowed me time off my teaching duties to finish up my revision of the thesis. Dr John Iliffe, before he left for Cambridge, England, encouraged me to publish this study and he and Dr John MacKracken read parts of my text and made useful criticisms and comments.

To the rest of my colleagues at Dar es Salaam I am grateful for their encouragement.

I am grateful to the Kenya Historical Association for inviting me to read revised versions of two of the chapters of this manuscript. In particular I am grateful to its President, Professor Bethwell A. Ogot, for his incisive comments and criticisms. Slightly different versions of two of the chapters have appeared in *Hadith* and I am grateful to the East African Publishing House, Nairobi, for permission to include them here.

Thirdly, I am greatly indebted to Dr Oliver Furley of Makerere University, Dr Jack Mitchell and Grant Kamenju of the Department of Literature University of Dar es Salaam and Miss Charlotte Morgan of University of Columbia for their editorial help. Mr Grant Kamenju like many of my Kenyan friends introduced me to some of the local sayings and proverbs, many of which were used to describe the missionaries. Certainly the results of this research would have been different were it not for the generosity given me by many Kenyans who so kindly answered many of my irritating questions during the period of my research in Kenya. None of these is responsible, however, for the conclusions and shortcomings of this study for which I alone am responsible.

Research for the original work was carried out in Britain and Kenya and I am deeply indebted to the archivists and librarians who helped me in all sorts of ways in securing the materials I needed.

Thanks for financial assistance for my research are due in greatest part to the Department of History and the Faculty of Graduate Studies, University of Alberta, Edmonton, the then University College, Dar es Salaam, Tanzania and the Department of External Aid, Canada, which financed my stay in Canada for six months to finish and present my original thesis. The Faculty of Graduate Studies, upon the recommendations of the Department of History at Alberta awarded me a Dissertation Fellowship which enabled me to do my research in Britain during the academic year 1965–66. The University College, Dar es Salaam, financed most of my research in Kenya under the University of East Africa Special Lectureship Scheme. I am also very grateful to the Research and Publication Committee of the then University College, Dar es Salaam, which helped to finance the rest of my research in Kenya. I would like to express my deepest gratitude to the Chairman of the Committee, Dr Wilbert Chagula, the then Principal of the College but now the Minister of Water Development and Power in the Government of the United Republic of Tanzania.

Dar es Salaam   A. J. Temu
January 1972

Introduction

Modern Christian work in what is today Kenya began in 1844. Johann Ludwig Krapf, a German trained at Basel Protestant Institution, working under the Church Missionary Society (CMS), established himself at Mombasa, on the east coast of Africa,[1] although this was an unexpected missionary establishment, and was not originally intended to be a permanent one. Krapf had been at Shoa, in Ethiopia, where he had joined the Abyssinian Mission. The Galla there proved to be too hostile to Christian missionaries and the CMS work therefore ended, with the CMS missionaries abandoning their station in 1843. Krapf went southwards to Mombasa from where he hoped to approach the Galla. The Europeans on the coast were friendly, as was also the Sultan of Zanzibar, who permitted Krapf to start a mission at Mombasa. With so encouraging a reception, he was undoubtedly optimistic of good results, and so he decided to establish his first mission in Mombasa, hoping from there to reach the Galla. Two years later, Krapf was joined by a fellow German, Johannes Rebmann, also sent out by the CMS. They moved from Mombasa, a predominantly Muslim town and by no means friendly, and established the first CMS station at Rabai Mpia, among the Nyika, now commonly known as Mijikenda people, fifteen miles from this Swahili-Arab town.[2]

This was not, however, the first time that Missionaries from western Europe had established themselves at Mombasa. Roman Catholic missionaries from Portugal were at work here for a short period during the occupation of the east coast by the Portuguese, in the sixteenth and seventeenth centuries. In 1597, Augustinian friars established a monastery at Mombasa, and about the same time, began work further north at Faza and Lamu.[3]

Roman Catholic occupation of the coast was part of the commercial expansion of Portugal into the Indian Ocean, in the two centuries following the discovery of a sea route to India by Vasco da Gama in 1497.

In this expansion, Mombasa was a backwater, serving only as a stepping stone and restocking port for Goa and the Portuguese East Indian Empire. In the same way, the Augustinian friars' occupation of the area was also restricted to the coast. It was no wonder, then, that the Portuguese conquistadores, traders and missionaries confined themselves to the forts, and did not penetrate into the immediate interior.

Significantly, Mombasa came to hold the same position in the modern period during the political and missionary occupation of Kenya after 1900. Once missionaries began work in the Kenya highlands, emphasis shifted and work on the predominantly Muslim coast became secondary to the work in Kenya.

The Portuguese found Arab-African settlements on the east coast. The most important of these city states were Pate, Malindi, Mombasa, and Kilwa, whose inhabitants, the Swahili-Arabs, were predominantly Muslim. Except for Malindi which saw a possibility of alliance with the intruders against Mombasa, the coastal settlements became very hostile to the Portuguese intruders and put up very strong resistance against them. In the face of this hostility the Augustinian friars acted cautiously and refrained from spreading Christianity to them openly. Indeed they confined themselves mostly to Fort Jesus where they made converts from among the slaves and employees of the Portuguese. Their work here was shortlived, for this seemingly unimportant venture came to an abrupt end in 1631.

The friars had sent Yusuf Hassan, a Muslim, to Goa where having been educated into Christianity, he was baptised and took the name of Don Jerome Chingulia. The friars made him ruler of Mombasa, Malindi and Pate in 1626, partly with the belief that they had found their agent and collaborator and partly in recompense for the murder in 1614 of his father, the Sultan of Mombasa.[4] However, Chingulia had remained true to Islam, a religion which his people embraced. In 1631 he organised a successful attack on the fort and killed all the Portuguese who refused to become Muslims. Boxer tells us:

The only survivors of Mombasa's little European community were one gunner who apostalised and four Portuguese laymen and an Augustinian friar who managed to steal away in a canoe and reach the Bajun Islands.[5]

Don Jeronimo, who had now taken his Muslim name, Yusuf bin Hassan, did not succeed in raising the whole of the East African coast against the Portuguese as he had planned to do. Personal rivalry between the city states still ranked high, and Zanzibar and the Bajun Islands remained loyal to the Portuguese. There was, however, little doubt that the revolt initiated a period of intermittent rebellion and chaos on the east coast. This attack led to the final overthrow of the Portuguese along the whole of the east coast in 1689 by a combination of local forces and forces from Oman in Arabia.

Certainly the rebellion of 1631 marked the end of the first phase of the introduction of Christianity at Mombasa. The few Christians who survived were overpowered by Islam which was, at any rate, more in accord with the customs and traditions of the coast than Christianity could ever be. Thus the Roman Catholic Christians disappeared from our literature of the coast and, in 1844, Krapf did not find any trace of these Roman Catholic converts. It was not until the nineteenth century that Christianity began to have some influence on the people of the Kenya coast, and then it was pioneered by Protestant missionaries. During the intervening period Islam was predominant on the coast, and was to continue to be so during the modern era of missionary expansion into Kenya.

Between 1844 and 1874 the CMS missionaries, who had been joined there by members of the United Free Methodists in the 1860s, achieved nothing by way of conversions. Sir Bartle Frere, who visited Rabai in 1873 censured Rebmann for the rigidity he had adopted in spreading the gospel there, and in particular for not adopting industrial training on the mission station as a means of spreading Christianity. On the results of the past three decades of missionary labour at Mombasa he reported that,

He found but eight converts at Kissuludini (Rabai) and five of

7

them belonged to two families which had joined from the African Orphanage at Nassik, near Bombay. Mr Rebmann has insuperable scruples regarding the admission of anything like an industrial or worldly element into the teaching or action of the mission.[6]

Whether this can be offset by the contribution to the geographical knowledge of the area the missionaries made to Europe which was utterly ignorant of the interior and of its peoples, it is not necessary to enter into here. Certainly, accompanied by Africans, they made several journeys into the interior and visited its peoples: Rebmann went to Kilimanjaro in 1848 and remarked of the centralised political system of Mandara's kingdom; Krapf visited Kimweri's court where he found Muslims already established. He also travelled down the coast as far as the River Ruvuma and commented on the flourishing commercial activity he found at every port he stopped at on his way, and in 1849 and 1851 he travelled into the interior of Kenya, reaching as far as Ukambani.[7] Mention must also be made of the work the missionaries did in studying African languages which they had to know in order to communicate with the Africans and to spread Christianity.

From 1874 until the end of the century the British Protestant missions worked mainly on the coast. During that period, their work, especially that of the CMS, was confined to freed slaves. In 1874 the CMS founded Freretown as a free slave settlement. Apart from the problems of the rehabilitation of freed slaves, the survival of the missions was uncertain. They were set upon the predominantly Muslim coast, where the population was just as opposed to them as the missions were to the established culture, law and customs. Inevitably a major part of the missionaries' work and activities, for most of the rest of the nineteenth century, was directed at survival among the Swahili-Arabs.

Inland from the Muslim coast, the territory was predominantly African. The Africans had no wish to become Christians, but they allowed the missionaries to live among them both for economic reasons and for the prestige and military strength that an alliance with the newcomers would bring them. The missionaries were entirely dependent upon the Africans for their safety, food and shelter, and were almost completely subservient to them.

With the establishment of British rule in Kenya, during the

second half of the 1890s, the position of the missions also changed. The missionaries became part of the establishment, and their future in Kenya was henceforth assured. The new administration gave them the protection they needed to expand into the heavily-populated highlands (and to deal a final blow to slavery without fear of the coastal Arabs), while the Kenya-Uganda railway, begun in 1896 and completed in 1901, facilitated their occupation of the highlands. Their work was then concentrated on this area, while the Muslim coast became a secondary consideration.

The focal point of the missions was the mission-house, in which the missionaries gathered their converts in order to teach them western civilisation and Christianity. Education, rather than Christianity, attracted Africans to the mission-houses after the First World War. By the mid-1920s the demand for education among the Africans had become widespread, and the means and conditions of the missions proved utterly inadequate to meet this demand.

The mission policy found its chief critics in a majority of Africans who had passed through the missions. Essentially, the missions taught and demanded submission and total obedience, neither of which could be reconciled with the rising nationalism of the Africans, led by the mission graduates. Politically, the missions became an adjunct of the administration, and although the settlers often did not like them and even despised them, they seemed from their actions to be more in sympathy with them than with the Africans whose interests they were supposed to serve. On the social scene, the missionaries maintained an essentially Victorian ethic, and they were violently opposed to African cultural nationalism. From 1925, different strands of disagreement betwen the missions and the Africans in Kikuyuland began to coalesce into a formidable opposition which found expression in the Kikuyu Central Association formed in 1925. Four years later a substantial number of Kikuyu made a break with the missions and set up independent schools and churches all over the highlands. These became ideological centres for the training of the Kikuyu who came to wage the nationalist struggle to regain Kenya's independence. Mission and government-controlled schools were aimed at producing Africans loyal to the colonial adminis-tration and to the ideology of the missions: indeed the so-called loyalists were a product of these mission and government schools while the forest fighters of the Mau Mau war, whose struggle led to the regaining of Kenya's independence, came from the African independent schools.

This work is a study of the policies and activities of the British Protestant missions in Kenya from 1874 to 1929. It is a modest attempt at a reinterpretation essentially aimed at putting the role of the missions in a new perspective within the context of the Kenya African society and its milieu, and especially the aspirations and expectations of the African peoples during that period.

NOTES

1. Krapf to Lay Secretary, January 10, 1844. CA5/MI.6, CMS Archives, London; and J. L. Krapf, *Travels, Researches and Missionary Labours During an Eighteen Years' Residence in East Africa* (London, 1960), p. 129.
2. *Ibid.*
3. C. R. Boxer and Carlos de Azevodo, *Fort Jesus and the Portuguese in Mombasa 1593–1729* (London, 1960), pp. 29–30; and Roland Oliver and Gervase Mathew, (Eds), *History of East Africa* (Oxford, 1963), pp. 136–137.
4. *Ibid.*, pp. 34–35.
5. *Ibid.*
6. Bartle Frere to Granville April, 1873, E.o 84/1391 Public Records Office. (Hereafter noted as PRO).
7. Krapf, *op. cit.* 2–3 – 233; 310–311.

1

The Freed Slave Settlement and Relations with the Arabs, 1874-1890

More than any other missionary organisation in East Africa, the Church Missionary Society was concerned with the fate of the freed slaves. The Society began to campaign actively for the abolition of the East African slave trade in the 1860s[1] and at that time decided to establish a freed slave settlement on the east coast. A similar colony had been founded by philanthropists in Sierra Leone in 1778. In 1791 the Sierra Leone Company was formed by philanthropists and bankers to introduce commerce and Christianity into the colony.[2] The first freed slaves arrived from England in 1789. They were joined by others from Nova Scotia in 1792 and from the United States in 1800. In 1808 Sierra Leone became a Crown colony. The previous year, however, the Atlantic slave trade was abolished, and Sierra Leone became a home for those slaves who were liberated while on the Atlantic Ocean on their way to the New World.[3]

The CMS was founded in 1799 and among its founders were men who had taken a leading part in the formation of the Sierra Leone Company.[4] It was therefore natural that the CMS made it its first task to begin missionary work among the liberated slaves in Sierra Leone, and led the way for other missionary societies to follow. In 1804 the first missionaries of the CMS arrived in the colony.[5] Here the CMS hoped to form a nucleus of African evangelists and catechists to be the chief agents of Christianity to their tribesmen in the interior of West Africa. By 1873, when the East African slave trade was abolished, these agents had spread the gospel across West Africa. Samuel Crowther, a freed slave, was consecrated Bishop of the Niger pastorate in 1864.[6]

With this precedent, and especially after the success of the liberated slaves in the evangelisation of the interior of West Africa, the CMS felt confident of equal success in East Africa. Before 1873 slaves freed by the British naval cruisers patrolling the Indian Ocean were invariably turned over to the missions already in East Africa or to private individuals.[7] A large number of those who were freed were sent to India, then under British rule.[8] However, the British naval patrol ships were able to rescue only a few slaves from Arab dhows before 1873. In 1873, with the abolition of the East African slave trade, it became necessary to establish a freed slave settlement on the east coast to accommodate the large numbers of slaves who would be liberated. With the support of the British government, the CMS therefore began a freed slave settlement at Freretown, ten miles from Mombasa, in 1874.[9]

William Salt Price, for long the superintendent of the CMS Bombay mission at Sharanpur, where, among other things, he had a small colony of African Christians liberated while crossing the Indian Ocean, was appointed the first superintendent. In 1875 the African Christians at Sharanpur moved to Freretown to help Price with the beginning of Freretown. Only about 150 young men and women returned to Freretown, having accepted the offer of the CMS Committee of free passage from Bombay to East Africa 'with a view to helping [Price] in one way or another to plant a freed slave colony in connection with [the] Mombasa Mission'.[10]

On his arrival at Freretown, Price secured land on which to settle the liberated slaves. In 1875 he was able to buy two hundred acres of fertile land from the local Arabs.[11] From the early days of Henry Ven, the CMS secretary at Salisbury Square from 1841 to 1872, the CMS aimed at making their overseas missions self-supporting and largely autonomous. Price, therefore, secured land for the freed slaves to subsist on and for the mission to grow crops.

Freretown was to be all things at once. First, it was to be a buffer and deterrent to any further slave trafficking from the interior; and then, of course, it was to be a training ground for future African evangelists and catechists who, like the liberated slaves in Sierra Leone, were to spread Christianity to the interior of Kenya and East Africa. Of the choice of Freretown, Edward Hutchinson had said that it should be sufficiently near the inland slave trade to permit an influence for good to radiate among the slave-collecting tribes and at the same time command a sufficient extent of territory to utilise to the utmost the labour stored up in such a settlement. A settlement so selected might, in the near future, become a self-supporting organised community.[12]

For the internal administration of the colony, Price was to serve as a civil and spiritual head; he assumed the role of the chief, or Wali, and the settlers looked to him for economic support, for law and order—he set up a small police force—and for military support.[13] This independent mission colony was to exist in the middle of the predominantly Muslim coast around Mombasa, but it was to be independent from the jurisdiction of the Wali of Mombasa, its civil head.[14] Later mission stations formed after 1874 (between 1874 and 1890 there were about eight) on the Mombasa coast also became independent mission colonies with their own administration and systems of government that differed markedly from both those of the Arabs on the coast and those of the tribes a short distance inland.

In 1876 Price left Freretown for England and J. A. Lamb from the Yoruba mission on the West coast succeeded him. At the same time the CMS established the post of lay superintendent at Freretown to look after the secular work of the settlement, to supervise cultivation and to adjudicate and punish offenders.[15] All missionary superintendents in the various mission stations performed the same function. As heads of the stations they dispensed justice. However, outside the colonies, their judicial functions were not recognised by either the Council of Elders, the administrative and judicial authority of the tribes near to the coast, or the Wali who ruled the Muslim population of Mombasa.

Once land was secured and an instrument of law and order was instituted at Freretown, there began both the work of receiving and resettling the freed slaves, and the main task of expansion along the coast and into the interior of Kenya. The first large batch of liberated slaves were received at Freretown almost immediately. With the help of the Africans from Bombay, better known as Bombay Africans, the missionaries put the adults to work and the young ones to school while those who were ill were taken care of until they were well.[16] From a small population of under two hundred in 1874–1875, the population reached over three thousand by 1890.

Some of the land the mission had purchased was reserved for the families of the freed slaves to whom the mission gave plots of land on which to subsist in order to be independent. The CMS took care of them only temporarily, for once they were given the land they were no longer expected to rely on the mission for their subsistence. The adults, however, were required to spend a good deal of their time providing the mission with labour on mission land and in the houses and gardens of the resident European missionaries. The CMS experimented with all sorts of crops in an attempt to find means of becoming self-supporting. The mission tried to grow coffee, coconuts, cereals and rubber but the climate on the coast was not suitable for this kind of agriculture.

The freed slave settlement presented the missionaries with the greatest problem of administration. Here many hundreds of liberated slaves, uprooted from their tribal authority from their early youth, were settled after they had been rescued from the Arabs. While they were slaves they often changed hands and could not therefore enjoy a settled life under a coherent legal system. The first challenge to the missionaries was to resettle them into an orderly community where there were laws to obey and organised work to do.

The second group of settlers to join the mission station were misfits and exiles from their own tribal society in the interior. These presented as many problems as the freed slaves, for they were social outcasts whose resettlement and rehabilitation was more a job for a modern, well-qualified social worker than for a single missionary whose main concern was the evangelisation of many thousands of souls in the interior of Kenya. Like the liberated slaves, they needed supervision, which the missionaries could not provide efficiently without neglecting their major task. In 1878 William Jones, the African pastor, complained that he was so pressed with secular work in settling minor cases that he could hardly find time to do pastoral work among the Wanyika.[17] Chauncey Maples of the Universities Mission to Central Africa (UMCA) at Newalla in Southern Tanganyika put the problems of association with the freed slaves at Masasi dramatically:

Upon the whole ... the presence of the returned slave com-

14

munity retarded rather than assisted the work among the tribes. Our great difficulty ... at Masasi ... was this. We had to take care of a number of worthless people who not only were not Christians but whose conduct was so bad that there was scarcely any hope of their ever becoming Christians: meanwhile their misdoings, quarrels, and excesses of all kinds took up an untold amount of time, as day after day I had to listen to their disputes and mete out satisfaction to the parties injured by them.[18]

The first thing that the missionaries did with freed slaves, run-away slaves or refugees from the nearby tribes was to baptise them. This was the condition the missionaries made for residence in their mission stations. Baptism for the freed slaves or the Africans was no indication of conversion on their part. Most of the Africans agreed to be baptised because they were attracted by the material comforts and wealth of the missions.

Dawnes Shaw, CMS missionary at Freretown, was later to remark caustically in 1886 that the settlers professed Christianity because the mission was the source of income, and the settlers often believed they were paid because they were Christians.[19] The Arabs and the Nyika also believed that the missionaries were at Mombasa mainly to support released slaves, for which purpose the Home Committee sent the mission large sums of money.[20] This belief had serious repercussions for the missionary work among the African people, for they associated Christianity with wealth. Most missionaries could not dispute the fact that they often bribed the Africans to make converts out of them. However, it was not necessary for them to bribe the freed slaves since they could, and often did, use other means to force them to become Christians. Apart from this situation, the missionaries on the coast —and this was more the case at Rabai and Freretown than else-where—were over-zealous about gaining converts. They were misled by the number of freed slaves they had baptised, and were wrongly convinced that the baptism would make the converts genuine Christians. It is easy to understand why William Jones, the African catechist, was more concerned in protecting his fellow Africans than in genuine conversion. As baptism was a condition of settle-ment on the mission, Jones readily performed the rite to ensure the slaves' escape from Arab slavers.

The missionaries at Mombasa administered the freed slave settlements with an iron hand and ruthlessly punished even minor offenders. The unruly behaviour of some of the freed slaves at Freretown certainly warranted mild punishment or even such serious punishment as was within the legal province of the superintendent. For example, as a civil overseer of the settlements, he had the power, in consultation with the others, to punish the young within reasonable limits; he could cane them much as African parents did their children. As for the adults, it was certainly within the superintendent's power to fine offenders and to withdraw privileges from them. But two lay superintendents, Commander W. Russell (1876-1877)[21] and J. R. Streeter (1877-1881)[22] went far beyond this, flogging and imprisoning offenders with brutality far exceeding that of the Arab masters to their slaves.[23]

In 1878 F. E. Wingram, the Secretary of the CMS, had ruled that missionaries could only flog or imprison offenders as a last resort and then only very rarely.[24] However, J. R. Streeter at Mombasa, A. Menzies, the missionary in charge, and schoolmaster J. W. Handford believed and acted contrary to the view held at Salisbury Square. They argued that flogging and imprisonment could best reform the sinful African, that the barbarism and heathenism of the African could be changed only by such heavy punishments, and that they were punishing the flesh so that the souls of their patients might be cured. Menzies pointed out that such heavy punishments had been justified by the results so far obtained:

It is very important to be rightly informed as to the desperate character of some of those who were beaten to see that their punishment was a stern necessity and also that in very many instances the punishment has been followed by complete reformation.[25]

The Blantyre Mission of the Church of Scotland (CSM) was similarly notable for its brutality in punishing cases of theft, lying, rape and drunkenness, and sometimes went to the extent of sentencing offenders to death. European travellers drew the attention of the British public to these brutalities. Bishop Edward Steere had written in 1882 to warn the missionaries of the UMCA at Masasi against usurping the power and jurisdiction of the legally constituted tribal authorities and undermining the confidence of the Africans in them.[26] The length to which the pioneer missionaries went to give themselves judicial and magisterial powers in areas where there were legally constituted tribal authorities is inexcusable as it cannot be argued that they were filling a judical vacuum or that they were providing peace where anarchy reigned. Tribal authorities did sentence offenders to death but only in very serious cases such as murder, and certainly not for lesser offences which the CMS and the CSM at Blantyre would have considered to merit the death penalty. The missionaries posed as chiefs but in their excess of evangelical zeal, not bothering to learn how these chiefs ruled, became more ruthless than the worst of chiefs.

But it was more the usurpation by J. R. Streeter, the superintendent of Freretown, of the power and jurisdiction of the Wali of Mombasa over the Arabs and of the Arabs over the slaves rather than the malpractices in the internal administration of the settlements, that caused the missionaries the most trouble with the Arab authorities and precipitated an inquiry into the administration of the mission in 1881. The Arabs and the Swahili, already incensed with the presence of the missionaries and the day-to-day attraction that they offered to the slaves to run away, found good cause to accuse them of the usurpation of the power of the Wali. From 1878 to 1880 Streeter had flogged and imprisoned not only people on the settlement but also slaves and a few Arabs outside the settlement, probably on the pretext that they had entered the settlement and committed some offence. The Wali and his elders protested and accused the superintendent of usurping their authority.

In 1881 the Sultan appealed to the Consul,[27] Sir John Kirk, to investigate the charges brought by his citizens against the missionaries, who were British citizens. Frederick Holmwood, the Vice-Consul, accompanied by Captain Mather Byles, went to Mombasa to investigate the charges.

The evidence produced before the commissioners at an open hearing attended by the Wali and his Arab elders and by the missionaries, Streeter and Menzies, proved that Streeter had inflicted physical injuries on the citizens of the Sultan. He was therefore guilty of having usurped the power of the Wali over his citizens, for which a civil suit could be brought against him. However, Holmwood persuaded the Wali and the Arab elders to settle the case out of court.[28]

But the case against the missionaries did not rest here. The

Bombay Africans at the mission had suffered indiscriminate punishment although they were often innocent; this was probably done to silence them since they were the most articulate and politically conscious of the settlers. They provided a more serious threat in that they were an educated class of Africans, and knew that the superintendent had no magisterial powers. In 1881 Tom Smith, a Bombay African artisan at Freretown, whom Streeter had flogged and imprisoned together with others, female and male alike, took the opportunity of the inquiry and petitioned Holmwood to enquire into the cruelties and malpractices in the administration of Freretown.[29] He pointed out that the missionaries, Streeter especially, had assumed magisterial powers outside their judisdiction as administrators of the mission station. To be sure the Arabs had drawn the attention of the commissioners to the malpractices in the administration of the settlement. They pointed out that an inquiry there would reveal matters far worse than hitherto brought to light.[30] The Rev A. Menzies reported:

> He [Tom] was on board the next day, early, and furnished the Consul with the names of all who had been beaten or imprisoned by Streeter within the past three years. He then told me, to my astonishment, that Mr Streeter was acting illegally in punishing the people as he held no magisterial powers.

The wonder is that the missionaries, although aware that the Bombay Africans were well-educated and articulate, assumed that they would not know of the social injustices and that the missionaries were acting illegally by sentencing them to prison or to be flogged. Streeter had earlier written to say that some of them were teachers and catechists, anxious for the welfare of their country;[32] nonetheless, he overlooked the possibility that they were aware of his injustices. Only Price consistently praised them for their help.[33]

The complaints of the Bombay Africans and the freed slaves were fully justified, as Holmwood and Mather Byles found, when they conducted an investigation into the mission station at Freretown immediately after the complaints were launched. Many of those who were punished came forward to show the injuries done to them. Holmwood commented:

The ocular proofs as to the severity of these floggings ... greatly astonished and shocked us, and I must tell you [Streeter] that in cases where the slaves of the Arabs apply to our Agency showing such traces of illtreatment, the Sultan is at once asked to free the slaves on the grounds that persons inflicting such injustices are unfit to be instructed with the charge of human lives.[34]

Captain Mather Byles, who had accompanied Holmwood, was even more vocal. He wrote:

Since I have been on the East Indian Station I have been the means of freeing several fugitive slaves on account of ill-treatment by their masters, but none of them have been beaten as severely as the two men I saw at the Mission.[35]

On the coast the population was predominantly Muslim. The cultural and religious differences between the Muslim population and the missionaries with their mission enclaves were so sharp that violent open clashes were soon to occur. The Arab population and the Swahili Muslims became increasingly antagonistic towards the mission colonies in their midst. The Swahili-Arab slave dealers and the Arab aristocracy, whose economic well-being was dependent upon slave labour, had every reason to work against the missionaries. For one thing, their coming almost inevitably meant the end of the still flourishing slave trade in the interior, and of the slave labour upon which the economy of the Arabs was based. The end of slavery would certainly bring economic ruin to the Arabs.

Almost at once the missionaries at Mombasa began to preach against Islam and against slavery, both fundamental elements of the Arab culture. But of more immediate concern to the Arabs was the attraction of the mission stations for the Arabs' slaves on the coast. The missions did not make it a secret that they wanted slavery to be abolished. They did not even hide the fact that they offered shelter and homes to slaves running away from their Arab masters. They gave them land to cultivate and build on, and helped them to form alliances with women on the station, thus usurping the power of their Arab masters. Price noted in his journal on 21 December 1875:

Married fourteen couples of the freed slaves. The men and women were grouped apart, and then the men, as their names came up, were asked to name the objects of their choice. This, in most cases, they were unable to do, and there was nothing for it but the would-be husband to enter the charmed circle and lead off the object of his affection.[36]

The doors of the British Protestant missions at the coast were open not only to slaves running away from their Arab masters, but also to any African wanting to settle there and, in time, to become Christian. As for the Nyika, the cohesion of the kayas into which they were divided for administrative purposes was too tight and too lasting to allow any mass migrations to the mission stations.[37] It was no wonder that, save in exceptional cases, such as during the frequent famines, the only people who migrated into the mission stations during this period were either runaway slaves, tribal social misfits or political exiles.

The first real danger to the missions on the coast came from the Arabs. The Arabs began to lose their labour force, the slaves, to the missions, where the missionaries used them as a labour force while pretending that the work they did was free. The CMS especially used force to procure labour from the settlers for the development of their estates and gardens. They allowed them to settle, offered them protection and treated them when they became ill, only on condition that they became Christians and provided the labour force the missionaries often required. The Arabs could not understand why the missions, and those who supported them, believed that this form of slavery in the missions was any different from that from which they were rescuing the Africans. Worse still for the Arabs, the loss of the slaves led to the deterioration of their farms and the improvement of the mission estates. In 1880 Sir John Kirk found that a considerable piece of ground at Rabai was being cultivated by fugitive slaves while on the opposite ridge their former masters watched their own estates going to ruin.[38]

Most of the missionaries noticed an undercurrent of Arab opposition from the very beginning. In 1876 the CMS medical missionary at Freretown, W. E. Forster, reported:

We are continually mixed up with political matters, the Arabs and Swahili are strongly antagonistic.... The English government knows how matters at present are but keeps in the background; this colony is being used as a cat's-paw. . . . Oh, but let not the flag of Jesus be united to that of Herod.[39]

Again, Binns, reporting that they had a number of runaway slaves from the Giriama, wrote, 'their owners are incensed against me for allowing them to remain here and last week they came down to demand them. . . .'[40] Binns had further refused to force them out of the settlement. The threat of an attack on the mission by the disgruntled slave-owners seemed probable.

In 1883 the Arabs at Mombasa openly attacked the mission stations.[41] They began with an attack on Fulladoyo, Pentagoa, and Makongeni, all independent colonies of runaway slaves. Slaves running away from their Arab masters often formed their own independent settlements in the interior. Such colonies became more common after 1880 when the Consul General, Sir John Kirk, rebuked the missions for harbouring the runaway slaves from their Arab masters. The missions had agreed to refrain from doing so officially although, in fact, they continued to do so secretly. Nonetheless the doors of the missions were not so far open as they had been.

The first runaway slaves joined the Fulladoyo settlement in 1879; a few began to make their way to the interior and joined Mbaruk. Others, however, found their own leaders and moved into the interior to found independent settlements. Kirk said there had been formed, at various times, many such settlements of runaway slaves, some of which were recognised by the Sultan. The formation of such settlements certainly disproves later arguments by Arabophiles that the slaves would prefer to remain with their masters rather than gain their freedom. There is no record of the number in each of the settlements but there were at least half a dozen large independent settlements.[42] The runaway slaves preferred to venture into the interior rather than to live amidst often hostile tribesmen who, like the Giriama, might take the opportunity of enslaving them and selling them to the coast. Freedom for them was priceless.

The Arabs had explored all the legal channels open to them before they finally attacked the missions in 1883. Between 1879 and 1880 they had protested to the Wali of Mombasa that the missions were harbouring their slaves illegally and, further, that

the missionaries had handled them roughly and sometimes committed murder when individual slave owners went to them to
recover their slaves. It was no longer safe for an Arab to approach
the missions alone. The Wali of Mombasa made several representations to the Sultan on their behalf.[43] Early in October, 1879 he
had sent a certain Majid bin Jabr to see the Sultan in person
regarding their complaints. The climax was reached when the
Arabs and the representatives of the twelve leading Arab families
at Mombasa sent a memorandum to the Sultan. The memorial
read:

> Our servants have ... submitted to anything at the hands of the
> Christians who have beaten them, carried off their slaves—
> stopped the paths and taken fines and every day this is becoming
> more common. The elders and chiefs of the town went to the
> Christians to speak with them on the subject, they imagined
> that possibly they had an order from our master or from the
> Consul General. We are under you and your protection but the
> head of every one is full?[44]

Sir John Kirk came to Mombasa in 1880 to try to find a solution
to the problem. He held a *baraza* with the representatives of the
Arabs and the missions; Harry Binns and the lay superintendent,
Streeter, represented the CMS. Kirk had previously advised the
missions of the position of the slaves at Mombasa, blaming them
for harbouring the Arabs' slaves:

> I have before written so fully to Mr Streeter that no doubt can
> exist as to the view I take of the position which is that as the
> law now stands an Englishman has no right to retain fugitive
> slaves against the will of their owners and the Sultan's
> authorities, and that this being so it is cruel to induce those
> poor people to trust to a protection which we are not in a
> position to give.[45]

Each side had begun to make preparations for the impending
clash in 1879. The missionaries at Mombasa who had provoked
the Arabs were sure that the Arabs would attack them. They
began to drill and arm the settlers and stocked the stations with
ammunition. The missionaries hoped that all the slaves on the

22

coast would rise against their Arab and Swahili masters and shake
off slavery. Slave risings were common in the American slave-
owning states, and the missionaries on the east coast of Africa
took pains to publicise them among the Africans in the hope that
they would emulate the American slaves.[46] The uprising was to
begin at Freretown, from where the missionaries hoped it would
spread all along the coast. Streeter had a large white flag with the
word *uhuru* on it. This he kept open to view in his house, making
it known that when the slaves saw the flag displayed they were
to rise and join the mission station to fight for their freedom.[47] The
Arabs, of course, saw the flag and knew what it was meant for.
Kirk visited the mission stations around Mombasa in 1880 only
to report 'the mission houses ... partook more of the look of a
military barrack than the teaching of Christianity. Over the missionary's bed hung two revolvers, there were Sniders and cartridge
belt.'[48] At Rabai there was a force of Christian soldiers two hundred
strong and armed with bows and arrows. The missionaries
regularly stationed armed guards at convenient places on the road,
or sent them out at regular intervals to spy out any surprise
attack from the Arabs.[49]

The Arabs, of course, viewed the mobilisation with great alarm.
They rightly felt that they were in danger of a general slave
uprising all over the coast, a rising instigated and promoted by the
missionaries. The Arabs' alarm at such mobilisation was justified,
and preparation for self-defence became necessary, when a few of
their numbers, often innocent parties, were murdered by the
Africans on the mission stations. The Arabs, therefore, began
to put up military demonstrations in readiness for the impending
war, and the missionaries responded by 'erecting sandbags, bundles
of timber, and placing a twelve pound rocket in position for
defence.'[50] Obviously the missionaries were chiefly responsible
for the mounting crisis. The awareness of the missions about
the situation at Mombasa, and the incessant letters to the
press, the Consul General and, particularly, to the public in
England, however, awoke the reluctant civil authority to the
situation on the coast. It was more the mobilization of the missions than their physical armed strength that scared the Arabs and
put off, for five years, any such attack. This was another reason
why, even when they finally decided to attack the mission stations,
the Arabs began by attacking the defenceless colonies of runaway

slaves, and attacked Freretown, Rabai, Ribe and Jomvu, only after they had completely wiped out Fulladoyo in 1883.

The clash between the Arabs and the missions on the coast preceded the scramble for territory in East Africa by European powers by about a year. It also preceded by a year Arab resistance to alien European rule in East and Central Africa which, Roland Oliver says, was common and widespread in East Africa between 1884 and 1888.[51] Arab resistance to the coming of Europeans to East and Central Africa was directed first against the missions whose difference in culture inevitably brought them into an open conflict and, second, against the British companies established to trade in the area. The open clashes in the area around Lakes Nyasa and Tanganyika (in the present Malawi and mainland Tanzania) have been amply documented,[52] as have those in Buganda and west-central Tanganyika.[53]

Of particular concern in this study are the events that took place around Mombasa, beginning with the Arab attack on the mission stations and the independent settlements of runaway slaves in 1883. Here we are particularly concerned with the actions and the role of the missionaries in precipitating the clash. The ill-feeling and hostility of the Arab population to the missions bear witness even more spectacularly to the general situation. But here the seeds of hatred between them had been sown early, in 1874, when the presence of the missionaries and of the Freretown freed slaves settlement began to undermine the basis upon which the economy and culture of the Arab society was founded. The mission stations heralded the end of slavery and, more immediately, began to drain the Arab plantations of their slaves. This was, therefore, a clash between two sharply different cultures, one believing in slavery and the other sharply opposed to it.

Oliver, summing up the situation in East and Central Africa, wrote:

> by 1888 the missions were everywhere threatened, in many places driven out . . . by commercial freebooters from Zanzibar and Oman who were making a last desperate bid to keep their domination in East Africa.[54]

This was certainly true of the mainland. But at Mombasa it was more the Arab plantation owners whose farm labour the missions were attracting and using who precipitated the clash. The letters of the Arabs to the Wali and their complaints to John Kirk and Holmwood in 1881 do not bring out the fact that their ivory trade had been threatened. Rather, it was the loss of slave labour, without which their economy would be completely ruined, of which they complained.

The Arabs' fear of European occupation of their territory, which they blamed the missionaries for initiating, assumed greater significance with the increase of European activities at Zanzibar; in particular the formation of the German East African Company in 1884. In 1885 the Germans obtained the support of the British in forcing the Sultan to agree to their claim for the mainland territory which the German company planned to occupy and develop commercially. The Arabs of Mombasa were even more surprised when the two powers ignored the Sultan's claim and divided the East African coast between them in 1886. Since 1832, when he had established his capital at Zanzibar, the Sultan had received British support. Support for native rulers in Africa was generally the policy of the British government during the period up to 1885.

However, the support for the German claim over Tanganyika in 1885 signified a sharp change in British policy over the area and toward Zanzibar. This was made evident the following year when, under the Anglo-German agreement, the coast was divided between them. In 1888 Lord Salisbury, the Conservative prime minister, gave a charter to the Imperial British East Africa Company (IBEAC) formed the previous year by William MacKinnon. The division of the mainland of East Africa between Britain and Germany was completed in 1890 when the line drawn by the two powers in 1886, as a boundary of their spheres of influence, was extended west of Lake Victoria to place Uganda under British rule. The British-controlled area was placed under the Imperial British East Africa Company (IBEAC) which took over the jurisdiction of the territory in 1888.

Almost simultaneously with the coming of the Europeans and the delimitation treaty of 1886, open Arab resistance spread across the coast. On the River Tana the Arabs, at Kao, attacked the United Methodist Free Church (UMFC) station at Golbanti in 1886.[55] The Swahili established at Jomvu seized the opportunity and closed all communication between Freretown and Rabai between

25

1887 and 1888, thus cutting supply lines and communication between them.[56] The missionaries answered by calling upon the British government to establish law and order, which meant occupation.

The Arabs placed the blame for the occupation of Mombasa on the Sultan. More important, of course, was the blame they levelled at the missionaries, who they seriously believed had paved the way for British acquisition of the coastal areas. On September 24 Price noted:

> Disquieting rumours come from Mombasa. The Arabs and Waswauli are angry with the Sultan for having sold them, as they say, to the English company. There are threats of attack from Freretown. The great fear is that slave traffic is doomed.[57]

In 1888 Arabs and Africans on the southern coast, in what became German East Africa, rose against the German company in defence of their territory.

The fear of the missions at Mombasa was that the Swahili-Arabs on the Mombasa coast would rally together and join their brothers on the southern coast and so form a combined effort to evict all Europeans from East Africa. The British had joined the Germans in the blockade and in so doing they increased the suspicion of the Arabs that the Europeans were united in their objective of controlling East Africa. This the missions at Mombasa had wanted to avoid, at least while things were so difficult for them.[58] Most of them, however, wanted British occupation, as it would give them peace and the protection they needed against the Arabs and the African chiefs. In 1885 the CMS officials in London recognised German interests in Tanganyika, as the Foreign Office had done, on the grounds that the German company would provide a permanent, fixed government there. However the Lay Secretary, Marshall Lang, emphasised that the CMS was not interested in political questions.[59]

The missionaries did their best to avoid becoming mixed up with the political activities of the British company, but they secretly rejoiced at its coming as it heralded the end of slavery and the power of the Muslims on the coast. This attitude was a great handicap in the evangelisation of the Africans, which was the main reason for the presence of the missionaries in East Africa.

At that time only neutrality could save the missions from destruction by the Arabs but it was not always easy for the missionaries to adopt a neutral policy in political matters. Moreover, the Arabs did not make a distinction between the missionaries and the agents of the company, believing that the missionaries and the company agents were allies and that they were working together to undermine the influence and power of the Arabs on the coast.

The feared uprising of the Arabs at Mombasa did not follow close by upon the uprising on the southern coast that broke out in 1888. In 1889 Hamis Khombo, a militant Arab opponent of the Europeans, and a descendant of the seven tribes at Mombasa, urged all the other coast chiefs to combine with their Arab brothers to the south to drive the Europeans into the sea. His urgings met with no response. Most of the leaders of the Arab uprising on the southern coast had been hanged and those at Mombasa, unsure of success or even of near-unanimous support over the coast, decided to postpone the uprising to the distant future when they could be more sure of success.

The British company, on the other hand, decided to conciliate their feelings as best they could, and followed a policy of 'peaceful penetration and lavish expenditure in presents and cash'[60] which helped merely to postpone the clash since the Africans and Arabs on the coast regarded the company as weak. 'It cannot be disputed,' wrote Jackson, 'that it fostered the belief that the 'Kumpuni' possessed a very large stock of watches, swords, clothes, etc. and an inexhaustible supply of cash.[61]

Mackenzie, the first administrator of IBEAC, knew that the situation on the coast was so tense that only the reconciliation of the Arab-Swahili slave owners could pave the way for the smooth administration of the company on the coast, save the missionaries from destruction, and bring peace. IBEAC's list of investors would certainly have aggravated the feelings of the Arabs, for many of them were philantropists and ardent emancipators. Still more aggravating to them would have been the charter of the company which included the aim of abolishing slavery and the slave trade.

The burning issue of the time demanding the serious attention of the company's directors was the problem of runaway slaves. Writing on October 17, 1888, a few days after the IBEAC had been given a charter, Euan Smith, the Consul General at Zanzibar, warned:

> There is a rapidly approaching crisis in Zanzibar and in coast affairs. . . . Whether [it is] at Rabai, Fulladoyo or Ribe is really of no consequence. The Arabs know no difference between the various denominations of missionaries. The knowledge that within easy distance of their homes there is one or more place of refuge where their runaway slaves can . . . as a matter of fact do find a safe refuge; and that those places . . . are under the protection of the British flag, and that they, the Arabs, are therefore powerless to attack them and search for their domestic slaves by force—this is sufficient to keep them in a state of irritation and hostility towards the missionaries.[62]

As a move toward a reconciliation with the Arabs, Mackenzie travelled all along the coast holding open-air meetings with the Arabs to hear their grievances. The Arabs immediately complained about the missionaries. William Jones wrote:

> The end of the year 1888 was a trying one for our station. As soon as the Imperial British Company came to Mombasa . . . the Arabs and Swahili . . . rose as one man, to complain of their slaves who had previously and at different times taken refuge in our mission stations. They demanded . . . that the missionaries should give up all the slaves . . . come down to the coast and all the slaves . . . should be made over to their masters after which the company would be allowed to have a footing in Mombasa.[63]

The company could not return the slaves to slavery again without incurring the wrath of the British public, still actively humanitarian, and infringing an important clause of its charter dealing wth the abolition of slavery and the slave trade. Besides, the missionaries at Mombasa would oppose the company and organise the settlements against them. The freed slaves, many of whom, Price reported, had 'been there for several years, [had] been baptised and confirmed; [had] their own houses and shambas, wives and children',[64] would choose to fight rather than follow their masters to slavery again. William Jones, who was an ardent champion of their freedom, chose to resist rather than to give them up:

28

When Mr Mackenzie, General Mathews and the Arabs come to pick out their slaves, I shall prove myself a useless servant; I will not and I cannot hand these poor souls to their cruel and unmerciful masters. . . .[65]

The crisis did not result in an open clash. The Arabs reluctantly agreed to a compensation of £3 500 for a total of 1 400 slaves found in the mission stations.[66] While IBEAC paid £1 300 the CMS, helped by a donation from Foxwell Buxton, paid £1 200, the UMFC paid £200 and the British treasury contributed £800. This conciliated Arab feeling for a time.

The missions, for their part, agreed to refrain from receiving any more runaway slaves. The CMS agreed to drive out any refugee in their mission stations who had no freedom papers, and the society agreed to allow the Arabs to enter their stations to search for their slaves.[67] The Arabs, however, did not fail to see that behind the compensation scheme lay a solid alliance between the missions and the company. They believed that the power and wealth of the company was behind the missionaries and their teaching.

NOTES

1. Edward Hutchinson, *The Slave Trade of East Africa* (London, 1874), pp. 82–83.
2. Eugene Stock, *The History of the Church Missionary Society*, 4 vols. (London, 1899–1916), Vol. I, pp. 46, 94.
3. Arthur Porter, *Creoledom, A Study of the Development of Freetown Society* (London, 1963), pp. 10–11, 19–34.
4. Stock, I, pp. 63–70.
5. *Ibid.*, pp. 94–95, 156–157.
6. J. F. Ade Ajavi, *Christian Missions in Nigeria 1841–1891: The Making of a New Elite* (London, 1965), pp. 194–195.
7. Frere to Granville, April 5, 1873, FO 84/1390, PRO, London.
8. *CMS Proceedings*, 1860–1861, pp. 73–74.
9. Price to Wright, May 17, 1875, C A5/017, CMS Archives, London.
10. W. S. Price. Report to the Secretary, CMS on the 'Future Prospects of the East African Mission,' October 6, 1882, 03 A5/01, CMS Archives, London.
11. Stock, III, p. 85.
12. Hutchinson, pp. 86–87.
13. Roland Oliver, *The Missionary Factor in East Africa* (London, 1952), p. 51.
14. *Ibid.*
15. Stock, III, pp. 89–90.

16. Binns to Wright, November 2, 1878, C AS/MI-6, CMS Archives, London.
17. William Jones to Wright, October 10, 1878, CC A5/MI-6, CMS Archives, London.
18. Oliver, *The Missionary Factor in East Africa*, p. 65 footnote.
19. Shaw to Lang, December 9, 1886, G3 A5/04, CMS Archives, London.
20. *Ibid.*
21. Stock, III, p. 90.
22. *Ibid.*
23. Helmwood to Streeter, July 6, 1881, Enclosure 3 in Kirk to Granville, July 21, 1881, FO 84/1600, No. 289, PRO.
24. Wingram to Streeter, February 5, 1878, C A5/L2, CMS Archives, London.
25. Menzies to Stock, July 12, 1881, G3 A5/01, CMS Archives, London.
26. Bishop Steere to Chauncey Maples, May 10, 1882, Enclosure in *Price Report 1882*.

'No one can regret more than I do that any part of your management should be thought injudicious, and it is after all but a small part. However when attention is called to it, I have no choice but to forbid altogether all beating of women under your jurisdiction or by your order, and to forbid all receiving of secret accusations, and to warn you not to comment upon the work of other branches of the Mission. . . .

'As Missionaries we have the right of admitting to Church privileges and suspending or withdrawing them and ultimately of expulsion by final excommunication. In all this we ought to advise with the Clergy and Laity under us, but the ultimate authority is ours.

'Politically we have no right at all, and can only live in the country by the permission or sufferance of the people we find there. There can therefore be no formal administration of justice, or claim to independence or anything like making war. We must get such justice as we can and if our position becomes intolerable we must choose between becoming martyrs and leaving the place.'

27. Sultan of Zanzibar to Kirk, June 10, 1881, Enclosure 3 in Kirk to Granville July 20, 1881, FO 84/1600, PRO.
28. Holmwood to Dr Kirk, July 7, 1881, Enclosure 11 in Kirk to Granville, July 20, 1881, FO 84/1600, No. 288, PRO.
29. *Ibid.*
30. *Ibid.*
31. Menzies to Stock, July 12, 1881, G3 A5/01, CMS Archives, London.
32. Streeter to Hutchinson, June 21, 1881, G3 A5/027, CMS Archives, London.
33. Price Report, p. 5.
34. Holmwood to Streeter, July 6, 1881, Enclosure 3 in Kirk to Granville, July 21, 1881, FO 84/1600, PRO.
35. Captain Byles to Captain Brownrigg, July 12, 1881, Enclosure 4, *Ibid.*, PRO.

36. Stock, III, pp. 87–88, quoting Price Journal, record for December 21, 1875.
37. Spencer Trimingham, *Islam in East Africa* (Oxford, 1964), pp. 23–29.
38. Kirk to Granville, October 19, 1880, FO 84/1575, PRO.
39. Forster to Wright, Annual Report, April 30, 1876, C A5/MI-6, CMS Archives, London.
40. Binns to Wright, October 5, 1879, C A5/MI-6, CMS Archives, London.
41. Stock, III, p. 92.
42. Frederick Lugard, *The Rise of Our East African Empire*, 2 vols. (London, 1893), Vol. I, pp. 222–236 *passim*.
43. Governor of Mombasa to Sayyid Barghash, September 8, 1880, Enclosure 2 in Kirk to Granville, September 22, 1880, FO 84/1575, PRO.
44. Memorial from the Arabs and Twelve Families of Mombasa, Enclosure 1 in Kirk to Granville, September 22, 1880, FO 84/1575, PRO.
45. Kirk to Lord Salisbury, January 9, 1880, FO 84/1574, PRO.
46. Kirk to Granville, October 19, 1880, FO 84/1575, PRO.
47. *Ibid.*
48. Kirk to Granville, October 19, 1880, FO 84/1575, PRO.
49. *Ibid.*
50. *Ibid.*
51. Oliver, *The Missionary Factor in East Africa*, p. 116.
52. A. J. Hanna, *The Beginnings of Nyasaland and North-eastern Rhodesia, 1859–1895*, (Oxford, 1956), pp. 16–50, 79–105.
53. Oliver, *The Missionary Factor in East Africa*, pp. 110–114.
54. Oliver, *The Missionary Factor in East Africa*, p. 116.
55. E. S. Wakefield, *Thomas Wakefield, Missionary and Geographical Pioneer in East Equatorial Africa* (London, 1904), pp. 257–258.
56. *Ibid.*, p. 259.
57. William S. Price, *My Third Campaign in East Africa* (London, 1890), p. 161.
58. Price to Lang, February 15, 1889, G3 A5/05 CMS Archives, London.
59. Lang to Price, January 25, 1889, G3 A5/15, CMS Archives, London.
60. Frederick Jackson, *Early Days in East Africa* (London, 1930), p. 146.
61. *Ibid.*
62. Euan Smith to Granville, October 17, 1888, FO 84/1909, PRO
63. Jones to Lang, May 27, 1889, G3 A5/06, CMS Archives, London.
64. Price, p. 186.
65. Price, p. 197.
66. Price to Lang, December 22, 1888, G3 A5/05, CMS Archives, London.
67. Kirsop, p. 101.

2

Missionary Work and Expansion, 1874-1892

The Church Missionary Society and the United Methodist Free Church were able to begin work among the coastal tribes only in the 1880s. The political problems created by their presence, especially that of the CMS freed slave settlement in the middle of a predominantly Muslim area, made it impossible for them to expand into the interior immediately after 1875. The missionaries had also to explore the surrounding area and to establish workable relations with the African peoples before they could begin direct evangelical work among the Africans. They therefore began to survey sites and to travel among the Nyika as a first step towards expansion into the interior. Harry Binns made frequent visits into the Nyika country, as did James Lamb (1874–1876), J. W. Handford (1875–1886), William Jones (1874–1904), and George David (1874–1884).[1]

From their base at Ribe mission, established in 1862, Thomas Wakefield and Charles New, the UMFC pioneer missionaries to Kenya, made frequent journeys to Kilimanjaro and Usambara.[2] After 1875, however, they directed their efforts to the Tana River region. From about 1870 the missionaries of the two societies branched out in different directions; those of the CMS toward the Great Lakes and Kilimanjaro, and those of the UMFC toward the Tana River region, the home of the Galla and Pokomo. In 1871 Charles New had recommended to his mission that it begin work among the Chagga after he had visited Mandara, the chief of the Chagga at Moshi. But the Foreign Mission Committee of the UMFC suspended work in this area in 1874 because of the difficulties

Charles New encountered with the chief who, it was reported, handled him roughly and took most of his possessions, for which actions the Foreign Mission Committee protested to the Sultan of Zanzibar, but in vain.[3] About the same time they stopped work at the court of the friendly chief, Kimweri of Usambara, although the Committee was in favour of such work.

But the UMFC desired more to work among the Galla; this they felt to be a moral obligation laid on them by Ludwig Krapf, and because of this they neglected more likely areas like the Usambara, where the UMCA came to have brilliant success with the Shambala and the Bondei of Tanganyika. Thomas Wakefield, the UMFC pioneer missionary, considered the beginning of work among the Galla a necessary obligation of his mission, and directed all his efforts towards that goal. Joseph Kirsop, the biographer of the Rev. Robert Moss Ormeroid, for many years in charge of Golbanti mission, said that the UMFC established themselves at Ribe not primarily to work among the Wanyika but as a stepping stone to the Galla.[4] This was why Wakefield and New spent so much time and effort exploring the area between 1862 and 1884. The lack of success at Ribe which Wakefield lamented in 1872, after ten years of residence there, was, he believed, due to the scanty and scattered Nyika population. This, however, did not divert his efforts nor those of the Foreign Mission Committee from the mission to the Galla which was set up in 1878.

The Foreign Mission Committee responded cheerfully to Wakefield's report that the Galla were willing to have the mission established. The Committee resolved that

in the judgment of this Committee the labours of our missionaries in East Africa should be confined to the Galla country and that for the present no attempt should be made to commence a mission at Chagga.[5]

In 1884 Wakefield established a mission station on the River Tana at Golbanti which was within easy reach of Lamu, a prosperous coastal harbour on the Indian Ocean, serving the Northern coast. Golbanti became henceforth the centre of UMFC work in the area for the evangelisation of the Galla and also the Wapokomo, whom Wakefield estimated to number about 14 000. Here Wakefield acquired about 6 000 acres of land, mainly belonging to the Wapokomo who were living on the banks of the River Tana.

33

The CMS established its first mission station out of Freretown and Rabai at Teita in the Ndara hills in 1882.[6] Harry Binns had visited Teita in 1880 and had recommended the establishment of a mission there as a stepping-stone to Ukambani and south-westward to Chagga and Upare. Further away towards Kilimanjaro, which Binns believed was the next step from Teita, Mandara had written to Captain Russell, the CMS Superintendent at Freretown, in 1875 inviting the CMS to start work in his country.[7] But, as we shall discover, Mandara did not wish to become a Christian.

CMS missionaries were so preoccupied with Freretown affairs and with the shortage of men and finances that they shelved Mandara's invitation. Ten years later, in 1885, James Hannington, the first Bishop of East Equatorial Africa, visited Mandara and was much impressed with him. 'With the exception of Mirambo,' he wrote, 'I never met in the interior a shrewder or more enlightened chief.'[8]

To be sure the British Consul at Zanzibar, Sir John Kirk, urged the CMS to occupy Moshi and establish British influence at Kilimanjaro in order to set a prior claim for the British there. Bishop Hannington co-operated with Kirk in all the plans for the British occupation of Moshi, thus revealing that the CMS was concerned to advance British imperialism in East Africa,[9] thereby illustrating the willingness Captain Mathews was to go to Moshi, on behalf of the Sultan and the British Consul, to obtain treaties from him and from other tribes on the mountain in order to forestall the Germans. Another example of the co-operation between the British and the missionaries came to light: Mathews consulted with the bishop before he set out for Kilimanjaro in the spring. Immediately after his return with the Moshi treaties, purported to have been signed by Mandara, Hannington hastily sanctioned the occupation of Moshi by the CMS despite the knowledge that the Germans also had signed treaties with Mandara twelve days after Mathews had signed his.[10] Fitch and Wray arrived at the Court of Mandara in July, 1885, and found the Zanzibar flag flying there. Kirk participated in the plans fully, but the arrival of the two CMS missionaries was not immediately followed by activity in mission work, for this was not what Mandara had invited them to do.

The position of Mandara in this struggle by the European powers to take over his country and, ultimately, the whole of Kilimanjaro,

34

is significant. From first to last it was clear that he wanted to use them for his own advantage. He was able to play them off one against the other, and often got what he wanted. Wray, in reporting a conversation with him, wrote that Mandara said, 'The Sultan of Zanzibar wants my country, the Germans want my country, you want my country. Whoever wants my country must pay for it.'[11]

Up to 1885, on the eve of the scramble for Africa that subsequently led to the partition of East Africa by Europeans without the advice or desire of the Africans, the missions had not ventured into the Masailand on their way to Uganda. This was a shorter and more direct route than the long and unhealthy one across central Tanganyika used by travellers and missionaries for many years past. The Masai who had ravaged much of this area held the corridor to the interior: they had lived on cattle plundering for much of their lives and by the middle of the century they had established an unchallenged authority across the Kenya plateau as far as the coastal belt and southwards to central Tanganyika. This extensive Masai empire, however, was mainly a cattle kingdom and was far from being imperialistic.

Hitherto the Zanzibari traders had not dared go into their territory, for 'to go into the Masailand,'' wrote Dawson, 'is, in the opinion of the Zanzibaris, like going into a sort of inferno.[12] In 1878 William Jones, on his tour to the Duruma, a section of the Nyika, witnessed much of the destruction the Masai had done to the Nyika country. He branded them 'a common foe' and in a language characteristic of the white missionaries, said, 'all East Africa [needs] a mighty deliverer from the Masai.'[13] In African eyes, however, this fear of the Masai protected Kenya from European intrusion.

In 1885 Hannington put forward the case for the Masai route.[14] He believed that once the Masai threat was overcome the route would be much shorter and more convenient. Besides this he maintained that the opening of the route would open opportunities of employment to the CMS Christians and they could produce a well-trained staff of responsible headmen. The same year James Hannington took charge of the party that ventured across the Masai route to Uganda. He was murdered at Bungoma on Mwanga's instructions. His death, though tragic, reflects more the power of the African chiefs and elders in East Africa, and their desire to defend their country from the attack of outside powers than what the whites rhetorically labelled their barbarism and bloodthirstiness.

The story of European missionary activities during this pioneer period spectacularly reflects this power; it also clearly demonstrates the utter hopelessness of the missionaries before the Africans, even though they were later to pose as superior beings under the strong arm of the imperial power that was invading East Africa. Almost all the European travellers to East Africa in the nineteenth century wrote and complained of the barbarism of the Africans. For such travellers and writers the missionaries were a civilising agent and, indeed, they may have been so in many ways. Both the writers and the missionaries themselves condemned the frustration they suffered at the hands of the Africans whom they had come to civilise and redeem from savagery and heathenism, and hastily labelled any opposition from the Africans as unprovoked savagery, or worse. A close examination of the period reveals beyond doubt that the missionaries were able to survive only because they were treated well by the Africans.

As on the coast, so in Kenya, the first threat to the work of the missions came from the Arab and Swahili slave traders. These latter, who dealt mainly with the Nyka and the Akamba, were quick to discover that the entry of the missionaries into the area, hitherto their trading monopoly, would undercut their trade and their influence among the Africans. In 1879 Harry Binns, on his journey to Teita, discovered that the Swahili-Arab slave dealers had told the Teita all sorts of stories about the missionaries and had bribed them to keep the missionaries out of their country: [they] gave the people at the top of the mountain a present of cloth on condition that they would not allow us to come to their village.'[15] The Akamba, for long agents of slavers and ivory traders from the coast, associated the missionaries with the Arab-Swahili traders: 'at Marangua, a Kamba village, Binns was asked by the Akamba if he had come to buy slaves, cattle, ivory....'[16] Swahili traders, established at Jomvu mainly in order to trade with the Nyika and to supply the coast with slaves and ivory, closed the road between Freretown and Rabai in 1883 in an attempt to cut communication between the two mission stations and to force them out.[17] Further inland at Moshi, Arab-Swahili traders, who were already established at Mandara's court in the early seventies, persuaded Mandara to get the CMS out of his country in 1886.[18]

During this pioneer period the missionaries to Kenya found that the power of the chiefs and elders with whom they had to deal was very real and great. The coastal tribes, or those immediate to it, had no centralised tribal authorities but each tribe was divided into small independent administrative units either of the same families or, as in the case of the Nyika, the kaya. The kaya had grown up as a stockade where the Nyika lived together for defence against the Masai and Somali, but in essence it became an administrative unit, each one being quite different and independent from the other. The Nyika then were formed into nine kayas, each under a council of elders. Here on the coast the missionaries were disappointed and frustrated by the diverse and numerous tribal authorities with whom they had to negotiate and above all to whom they had to pay taxes.

The African chiefs, or elders, charged the missionaries a fee for permission to enter and reside among their people, or a transit fee to the next village. In 1865, on his first journey to Galla, Thomas Wakefield 'secured beads, brass, and iron wire, coloured cloth, grey and indigo-dyed calico, lemani (a coarse cloth) as presents to the chief and influential men.'[19] These were the currency of the Galla and Wakefield had to pay them to the Galla elders in order to get permission to travel about the country or to stay there. The Africans knew that their country was valued highly by the Europeans and so they demanded high fees. These varied from place to place; the Africans and the missionaries often bargained. In the early days it was the numerous tribal authorities to whom the missionaries had to pay satisfactory tax that caused frustration. Their meagre provisions were often insufficient for the elders on the coast. The missionaries therefore complained that the elders were the cause of their impoverishment. 'Big men and little men,' wrote Wakefield, ' demanded their *ada* of cloth until the missionaries were impoverished.'[20]

As the missionaries and European travellers journeyed more frequently across the country (this was especially so during the 1880s) the Africans rightly interpreted it as a great demand for the resources of their country and consequently began to demand more from the foreigners. In Kenya, both on the coast and in the interior, most of the Africans, and especially the elders whose duty it was to defend the people, were less aware that the missionaries were preparing a way for the occupation of their country by their fellow Europeans. The Arabs on the coast, however, had quickly discovered the alliance that was later to emerge between the missionaries and the imperialists of the British Company yet to be formed.

The main concern of the Africans for the time being was, therefore, to gain materially from the newcomers. The equipment and provisions of the pioneer missionaries undoubtedly encouraged the Africans to believe that the missionaries were rich and that they could therefore pay more in goods than previously. Thomas Wakefield's equipment on his journey to the Galla has already been cited. He was far from being poorly equipped. In 1885 Hannington carried with him a miscellaneous assortment of articles more or less bulky with which to purchase food, pay tribute, hire extra assistance and porters.'[21] Most missionaries were thus abundantly equipped; they also carried guns, had means to employ runners and, above all, their caravans numbered hundreds of men as well-equipped as any invading army.

The rise in what, today, we would call taxation and toll but which the missionaries wrongly called *hongo* (bribery) caused them great alarm and anxiety. Hannington expressed the fear that he did not carry enough to pay the Teita, Akamba, Kikuyu and Nandi on the way to Uganda through Kenya. There had been many instances where missionaries were refused permission to proceed with their journey unless they had paid what the Africans demanded. As early as 1871 Wakefield was forced to cut short his journey to the Galla at Kauma kaya because he would not pay the $100 which the elders demanded.[22] At Ukambani in 1885 Hannington was not allowed to proceed with his journey until he had paid the elders and fed the people, since famine had just struck the country.[23]

The problems the missionaries faced, once they were established at the court of Mandara, and at Teita, may be taken generally as characteristic of the whole situation in this period. The missionaries worked alone and depended upon the chief or the elders for their safety, food and accommodation. If anything went wrong they could seek redress only from the chief or elders of the village. They came to Moshi or to Teita, for example, to spread christianity and western civilisation to the Africans. The Africans interpreted their coming differently. The Galla, for example, believed that they had come to protect them from the incursions of the Masai, and the missionaries were permitted to stay there only on condition that they promised to do so.[24]

Mandara, who has been described as one of the greatest African diplomats of the time,[25] wanted the missionaries for political reasons. Mandara's greatest adversary at Kilimanjaro during his long reign, from 1870 to 1891, was Mangi Sina of Kobosho, another kingdom on the mountain west of Moshi.[26] Mandara therefore looked for an outside alliance to enhance his power, and found it with the Warusha, the greatest military power outside Kilimanjaro. Once Mandara won this alliance he was able to engage in campaigns against the Kirua, Kilema and Marangu on the eastern side of the mountain. Then he established relations with the Swahili-Arabs; this was primarily a trading link, but one that brought him into alliance with the Sultan of Zanzibar from whom he obtained guns and cloth. The third alliance was with Europeans, first the CMS missionaries, and then the German empire builders.

In 1885 Mandara allowed the CMS to establish a mission station at Moshi.[27] At the same time he concluded a political treaty with von Juhlke, representing the Germans, and so obtained the support of the two European powers concerned in the situation.

The fortunes of the CMS became precarious as soon as Mandara discovered that the missionaries could not supply him with the arms he needed or the political prestige that he associated with their presence at Moshi. The *Church Missionary Intelligencer* reported in 1885 that Mandara had

plainly said he [wanted] guns and artificers and European appliances. He [did] not want Christian teaching any more than Mutesa required it.[28]

In 1886 he closed the market where the missionaries obtained their food for five days, probably because they had given him neither the guns nor the political backing he wanted.[29] The Swahili traders at his court had become substantial in number and were persuading him to cut off the links he had established with the CMS. The interests of the Swahili and Mandara were the same since both were interested in the slave trade to which the CMS were bitterly opposed. Fitch wrote:

> The slave trade seems to be reviving in these parts, a band of Swahili dealers have been camped at Mnoray. Mandara obtains his slaves from Ugweno. To our arguments against it he pays no attention; to him the Swahili argument is better for it is backed by gunpowder and calico.[30]

It was no wonder then that up to 1887 he had not allowed the CMS to enrol any children in their school or shown any positive sign of his favour. There was, however, a change in Mandara's attitude about this time. He expressed the wish to learn the Bible and, more important for the CMS, he allowed them to enrol children in the school. But as this was also the time when the German East Africa Company established a station at Moshi, in August, 1887, Mandara was perhaps interested in playing off the CMS against the German company.

At Teita the CMS missionaries, J. A. Wray and W. Morris, suffered at the hands of the elders, as had the missionaries at the court of Mandara. Up to 1885 Wray, who had been there since the Teita mission was founded in 1882, had not succeeded in persuading the Teita to come to church or to allow their children to enrol in the school. The opposition of the Teita elders to the mission had been growing constantly. In 1885 and 1887 famine broke out all over the Nyika and this was their pretext for driving the missionaries out of their country. It was all right for the missionaries to stay as long as everything progressed well at Teita. In spite of the fact that Wray had organised food for them, their opposition to the missionaries reached fever pitch in 1887. Bishop Henry Parker had hoped that the Teita would look upon Wray as their friend because of the famine relief he had organised.[31] But on the contrary the Teita openly accused the CMS of causing the famine and began to attack them in an attempt to evict them from Teita. Morris reported that the Teita had made two surprise attacks on him and Wray in 1887. 'Then for some months,' he wrote, 'affairs continued in a very unsettled state owing to the absence of rain; for which we were blamed and threatened with another attack....'[32]

Wray and Morris were very disappointed with the attitude of

the Teita. They had organised famine relief, not because they felt responsible for the famine, as the Teita supposed, but because, as missionaries, they felt it their duty to rescue the tribe from starvation. In return they expected the Teita to be grateful to them and to attend church services. It was no wonder that Wray was disappointed when the Teita became more hostile to him:

> I have seen a good deal of hypocrisy among these [Teita] people but never any to equal that of today. Those very men who call themselves my friends were among my enemies. Others whom we had fed and protected at Rabai were among them and this is how they return kindness.[33]

What Wray said was typical of the attitude of most of the missionaries towards the Africans who did not readily respond to the new missionary teaching. Had the missionaries been in a position to force the Africans to submit to them they would certainly have done so. But the missionaries were living in the country of the Africans; their being allowed to stay in their midst was an act of generosity by the Africans. They were at cross-purposes about what each expected from the other. The missionaries wanted the Africans to become Christians; the African chiefs or elders, however, saw the missionaries as allies, and the rest of the Africans were only attracted to them because of their material wealth.

NOTES

1. *CMS Proceedings*, 1880/82, pp. 29–30.
2. Wakefield, 39, pp. 110–115.
3. The Foreign Missionary Committee (United Methodist Free Church) Minute Book I, p. 381. (Hereafter referred to as FMC [UMFC] Minute Book.)
4. Kirsop, p. 33.
5. FMC (UMFC) Minute Book I, p. 393.
6. Stock, II, p. 135 and III, p. 266.
7. Mandara to Captain Russell, 4th after Ramadan (sic), C A5/MI-5, CMS Archives, London.
8. Hannington to Wingram, April 21, 1885, G3 A5/02, CMS Archives, London.
9. Hannington to Wingram, February 14, 1885, G3 A5/02, CMS Archives, London.

10. Hannington to Wingram, February 14, 1885, G3 A5/02, CMS Archives, London.
11. Wray to Lang, September 19, 1885, G3 A5/02, CMS Archives, London.
12. Dawson, p. 381.
13. William Jones, 'Journey to Duruma,' August 7, 1878, C A5/014, CMS Archives, London.
14. Hannington to Wingram, April 21, 1885, G3 A5/02, CMS Archives, London.
15. Binns to Wright, September 9, 1878, C A5/MI-6, CMS Archives, London.
16. *Ibid.*
17. Wakefield, p. 179.
18. *Church Missionary Intelligencer*, 1885, pp. 515-516.
19. Wakefield, p. 47.
20. *Ibid.*, p. 58.
21. Dawson, p. 207.
22. Wakefield, p. 53.
23. Jones to Lang, Diary of Events, August 18, 1885, G3 A5/02, CMS Archives, London.
24. Wakefield, p. 55.
25. Cathleen Stahl, *History of the Chagga People of Kilimanjaro* (London, 1964), pp. 249–250.
26. Stahl, p. 245.
27. Hannington to Gentlement [sic], May 8, 1885, G3 M5/02, CMS Archives, London.
28. Dawson, p. 345.
29. *Church Missionary Intelligencer*, p. 515.
30. Fitch to Lang, January 2, 1886, G3 A5/04, CMS Archives, London.
31. Parker to Stock, March 3, 1887, G3 A5/04, CMS Archives, London.
32. *Extracts, Annual Letters (CMS)*, 1888–1889, pp. 18–19.
33. Wray to Lang, November 10, 1887, G3 A5/04, CMS Archives, London.

3

The Changing Situation and the Abolition of Slavery, 1890-1907

In 1890 there was a dramatic change in the affairs of East Africa. That year the Anglo-German treaty between Britain and Germany was signed in Berlin on July 1,[1] agreeing to a division of territory in East Africa. In 1886 they had defined their spheres of influence in East Africa from the Indian Ocean to the eastern edge of Lake Victoria. In 1890 the partition of East Africa was completed; the boundary line drawn from Vanga to east of Lake Victoria was extended westward across the lake to place Uganda under British influence. Under the same agreement Germany recognised a British protectorate over Zanzibar in exchange for Heligoland.

This was to be the first time that Africans were to yield their power and authority to foreign powers from outside East Africa. The Sultan of Zanzibar did not hold authority over the tribes in the interior—that is, the Masai, Akamba, Nyika, Galla, Somali, Kikuyu, Chagga and Pokomo.[2] The Masai, it is true, had been all-powerful in the interior from the middle of the century and had raided, almost freely, as far as down the coast as Mombasa itself.

On the coast the Sultan's flag certainly flew, but the coast towns were independent.[3] The flag was therefore more the sign of relationship with foreign powers than an indication of the power of the Sultan over the Arabs on the coast. The Mazrui family at Mombasa, for example, had not accepted the Sultan's sovereignty even after he had partially defeated them in 1837. Seyyid Khalifa succeeded in preventing Mbaruk bin Rashidi, the Mazrui leader at Mombasa, from leading a revolt of the Mombasa Arabs against him only by paying an annual subsidy.[4]

The first real threat to the power and influence of the Arabs at Mombasa, therefore, came from the British East Africa Company, which was chartered in 1888 to exploit the economic resources of the area, and which was to rule and administer the British sphere of influence.[5] The company established its base and headquarters at Mombasa which was also the centre of the Mazrui families on the northern coast. IBEAC's primary motive in East Africa was, of course, economic.[6] For the company to attain its goal it was necessary to compromise the political climate on the coast already made explosive by the missionary presence. Moreover, the events on the southern coast, where the Arabs had taken up arms in 1888–1889 to resist the German company, made IBEAC adopt a reconciliatory policy to avoid provoking the Arabs on the northern coast into rebellion. IBEAC therefore decided to interfere as little as possible with the affairs of the Arabs in their administration, laws and customs. For the whole period of the company's rule on the coast, 1888–1895, the coastal towns were independent and the administration of the towns was in the hands of the Walis and the Sheikhs.[7] By 1890 the company had stationed representatives in all the big towns at the coast: at Vanga, Malindi, Lamu, and up on the Tana River. But their main duty was the collection of customs. In 1895 Arthur Hardinge found that the Arab chiefs at Gazi and Takaungu had never been affected by the presence of the representative of the British company. He wrote:

The District Superintendent at Vanga and Malindi paid short visits to Mbaruk of Gazi and Salim of Takaungu but they found it necessary to ignore or affect not to be aware of the offences of both chiefs against the laws such as the slave dealings of the one and the imposition of taxes on British Indian subjects by the other.[8]

This policy, however, proved a great handicap to the missions and almost crippled their work between 1888 and 1890. In 1888 the company compensated the Arabs for the loss of their slaves to the missions in order to keep them from rising up against the missions and other Europeans, and thus undermining the success of the company in its infancy. The company's director, William Mackenzie, forced the missions to agree not to receive any more runaway slaves.[9] Almost immediately he discouraged the missions from doing gospel work on the coast and in 1899, when there were rumours that the missionaries were still giving refuge to runaway slaves, Mackenzie told the missionaries on the coast that they should either respect the laws of the country they had come to live in or

> if the same [were] distasteful to anyone coming [to the coast] the proper alternative is to go elsewhere and not jeopardise the good fellowship and possibly the lives of their fellow countrymen resident here.[10]

The Anglo-German treaty of 1890, however, brought a change. After 1890 the missionaries began to adopt a more militant policy towards the coast. With Zanzibar becoming a British protectorate that year, it is possible that the missionaries began to foresee that the political power and influence of the Sultan of Zanzibar and of the Arabs on the Mombasa coast would wane. In 1890 European powers with interests in Africa, together with the United States and Turkey, had signed the Brussels Act in which they had, among other things, committed themselves to the abolition of slavery in Africa. This made the missionaries at Mombasa more confident that the British government would back them in their campaign to root out this evil from the coast and to win the coastal population for Christ.

It was not until after 1890 that the CMS began evangelical work among the Muslim population at Mombasa. In 1893 the CMS invaded the town.[11] That year three women were sent from England especially to preach among the Muslim women of the town, as this, the CMS believed, was the best way of converting the Muslim population to Christianity. The Englishwomen established themselves at Ndia Kuu, then the main street of Mombasa.[12] About the same time W. E. Taylor, a medical missionary, established his residence close by. Taylor ran a small dispensary in which those who came for treatment had to listen to a gospel lesson before being treated. He reported that the main work of the woman missionaries 'consisted in personal dealing gained by visiting from house to house and in public preaching of the gospel and hymn singing.'[13] Arthur Hardinge, who was most opposed to direct evangelical work on so predominantly a Muslim coast, said,

45

the ladies of the mission partitioned the town into districts which they worked on the methods but with far more the zeal of the lady district visitor in an English parish.[14]

Some of the CMS missionaries and catechists at Freretown began to make frequent visits to Mombasa to hold services in the main market of the town and in open places where the Arabs or Swahili were likely to gather. The campaign of the CMS to win over Muslims at Mombasa reached its peak with the opening of a mission hall in 1896 by Alfred Tucker, the third bishop of the CMS East African Mission. Tucker said that the mission hall was built as a means of reaching the Muslim population '... and [as a means of carrying] on educational work among the Mohammedan children our main object being to win them for Christ.]'[15]

The Arabs at Mombasa were very disappointed with the missionaries for preaching against Islam. They believed that the missionaries were able to do so only because the British government was behind them. In 1896 Arthur Hardinge said:

As many of the Arabs passed through the market and heard the open-air preaching of the missionaries they [the Arabs], felt that but for their English rulers these priests would not dare to declaim in the public streets against the doctrines of their religion.[16]

Anti-European feelings among the Arab population increased with the invasion of the city by the CMS. By 1895 feelings were running so high that a clash was soon to occur. That year administrative responsibility for the area between the coast and the eastern shores of Lake Victoria passed from IBEAC to the British government and the area became known as the East African Protectorate. The Arabs all over the coast believed that this change would be followed immediately by the abolition of slavery. This particularly alarmed them since their hopes that the coastal strip, hitherto leased to the company by the Sultan, would revert to him or be given to themselves, were dashed to the ground. Hence there were the strong feelings this aroused giving the Arabs cause for rebellion.

The affairs of the missions too began to take a different turn. The change of authority from African to company rule which took place after 1888 meant a change in the relations between the missionaries and the African authorities. For one thing, it was no longer necessary for the missionaries to submit to the wishes of the African kings, chiefs, or elders. Nor did the changed conditions, especially after 1895, permit the chief to extract from the missions as much taxation as they wanted, for the missionaries could now refuse to pay and still go unmolested. A typical example of the change of attitude by the missionaries towards the African kings, chiefs and elders is spectacularly revealed in what Alfred Tucker, third bishop of East Equatorial Africa Mission, wrote only eight days after the Anglo-German treaty was signed:

We are going forth on our long journey [to Buganda] neither depending upon nor trusting in the arm of the flesh, nor courting the patronage of the world, much less that of an African potentate.[17]

Far away in the interior, at Moshi, the affairs of the CMS, already established at the court of Mandara since 1884, changed with the passing of the country into the hands of the German East Africa Company (1885 to 1890)[18] and the German imperial rule (1891 to 1919).[19] With a promise of protection from the German government, the CMS decided to stay at Moshi.

Reports on the affairs of Moshi from the CMS from 1888 to 1890 show the German hold on the mountain to have been precariously weak. Albert Steggal and E. A. Fitch, CMS missionaries at Moshi reported widespread hostility from Chagga chiefs to the Germans.[20] In 1890 Steggal reported that a German party that had hoisted the German flag at Machame, a Chagga chiefdom west of Moshi, had been captured by Sina of Kibosho and had been imprisoned for two days without food.[21] Sina attacked Machame and pulled down and burned the German flag.[22] Neither the Germans nor the CMS seemed to make headway with Mandara, and in 1888 the German agent at Moshi had planned to move from Moshi to a friendlier centre which would be more attractive to German colonists. The German agent had invited the CMS to move with him but the plans did not materialise because of hostilities against the Germans which broke out on the coast.[23] It was not until after 1890 that Germany gained a proper footing on the mountain. Hitherto the German East Africa Company was engaged in suppressing the uprising against them on the coast. By 1891 von Wissmann had completed the subjugation of the coast, from where he moved to Kilimanjaro, the next area of resistance, where the most powerful chief, Mangi Sina of Kibosho, had never accepted German company rule. In 1891 Sina was conquered and forced to sign a treaty.[24]

With the defeat of Sina of Kibosho in 1891 the Germans adopted a firmer policy towards the Chagga and began to suppress them with a cruelty that offended the missionaries of the CMS who excitedly began writing home of the cruelty of the Germans. This, and the underlying CMS sympathy for the Chagga provoked German action against the CMS.

Mandara had died and Meli, one of his sons, succeeded him.[25] Carl Peters, who had arrived to take charge of the German station at Moshi towards the latter part of 1891, decided to move his capital from Moshi to Marangu. The move from Moshi to Marangu was certainly more than the mere transference of a capital. For Chief Meli of Moshi this change meant a loss of influence with the Germans to the weaker and more envious Mangi Marealle of Marangu, whom he was planning to invade. Chief Petro Marealle, a grandson of Mangi Marealle, told the author that his grandfather formed an alliance with Carl Peters to avert the destruction of his kingdom by Meli.[26] The alliance between Marealle and Carl Peters became complete with the establishment of the German capital for the Kilimanjaro area at Marangu.

The CMS missionaries, who had hitherto remained on good terms with the Germans and who had perhaps been serving as intermediaries between the Germans and the chief, if not also exercising a restraining hand on both sides, then lost this role. It is possible that with the loss of their German friends the CMS missionaries naturally threw their whole weight on the side of the one authority remaining at Moshi, Chief Meli, on whom they still depended for their safety, food, and above all, for the success of their mission work among the Chagga at Moshi. This alienated them from Peters, who was thus given grounds for accusing the CMS of aiding Meli against them. This eventually led to the expulsion of the CMS from the German-controlled area.

Naturally Peters had reasons for wanting the CMS to move from the German sphere of action, especially since the missionaries had reported and protested at his ruthless actions towards the Chagga at Marangu. The CMS at Moshi far from the supervision of the administrators at Marangu were therefore not in an enviable position. Peters wanted to crush the Chagga who, he rightly believed, would not accept German rule without force of arms. By 1892, when Peters was replaced by von Bülow, the situation at Moshi was explosive, and the missionaries already feared that there would soon be murder and chaos on the mountain.

It was clear that Meli would not rest content while Marealle, in collaboration with the German administration, undermined his influence and prestige. Marealle, on his side, was determined to take advantage of his alliance with the Germans to arrange for the defeat of Meli, which he could not accomplish alone. The situation was further complicated by the fact that Meli had not succumbed to the German administration. Meli, like Sina of Kibosho or his father Mandara, could be brought to agree upon a treaty for German occupation of Moshi only by force of arms. This explosive situation was ripe for intrigue and Marealle took the opportunity to create the atmosphere in which the Germans attacked Meli from their base at Marangu.

Marealle arranged for a man named Mawalla to shoot a soldier whom von Bülow had entrusted with a letter to Meli. He planned for the murder to be carried out in Meli's own country, and Mawalla was to report to von Bülow that the murder had been perpetrated on the order of Meli. Marealle believed that von Bülow would react by sending a punitive expedition against Meli. Mawalla's grandson, Joseph Mawalla, and Petro Marealle have provided information to prove the truth of the plan although they disagree as to who carried out the murder.[27] What is important, however, is that the plan was executed as arranged by Marealle and the news delivered to von Bülow who then set out on his ill-fated punitive expedition against Meli in 1892, only to be killed with some German soldiers who accompanied him.[28] The German officers who escaped abandoned the Marangu post for the coast. Meli's success over the German force greatly enhanced his prestige and brought a change in the fortunes of Marealle, whom Meli was soon to attack.

But of serious consequence to the position of the CMS at Moshi was the fact that rumours soon spread that they had been involved in the fight and had supplied Meli with arms. It was also believed in German circles that one of the CMS missionaries had led the army that defeated von Bülow. Since Meli's force greatly outnumbered the German force, and was better armed, it is very unlikely that Meli needed help from the missionaries. It is still more unlikely that he needed a missionary to lead a force in unfamiliar terrain. To avert the impending trouble with the Germans, Steggal tried to seek a peaceful solution to the problems created by von Bülow's defeat and therefore acted as intermediary between Meli and the Germans.[29] Von Soden, the Governor, apparently wanted a peaceful solution also, if Meli would agree to a return to peace, compensation for property lost by the Germans and the re-establishment of a military force on the mountain.[30] It is unlikely that Meli would have agreed to yield to the German terms, which amounted to re-occupation. Meli, like his father Mandara, did not at all relish the occupation of the mountain by an alien power since this would have entailed the restoration of Marealle's power.

If Steggal had succeeded in persuading Meli to accept the re-occupation of Moshi by the Germans he would have certainly dispelled the belief, widely held by the German officials, that the two CMS missionaries at Moshi had helped to bring about the defeat of von Bülow. This would have helped to ease the tense atmosphere between the CMS and the Germans, and probably put off a second German expedition against Moshi for some time.

Failure to achieve a peaceful solution with Meli led to the dispatch to Kilimanjaro of a strong army under von Schele from the German headquarters at the coast. With the help of eight hundred Kibosho warriors and provisions from Marealle, the German force defeated Meli and finally forced him to come to terms in September 1892.[31] Von Soden, Governor of what was then German East Africa, believed that in the interests of Germany and of peace on the mountain the CMS had to move out of Moshi. Under heavy pressure the CMS reluctantly moved, establishing themselves at Taveta in Kenya, not far from Moshi.

The role of the CMS at Moshi in the political activities of the Chagga came to an end in September 1892. The involvement of the missionaries in the activities of Mandara and, after 1891, in those of Meli and the Chagga is in itself a very interesting episode. The CMS wavered in its support of Meli. When Steggal advised

Meli to accept German re-occupation of Moshi in 1892 it may well be that he knew that this was bound to come, but it was more the interests of the mission that determined the line he pursued than the interests of Meli or the Chagga.

The withdrawal of the CMS from Moshi came at a time when the society was also campaigning for the annexation of Uganda by the British. This campaign, which has been fully documented elsewhere, culminated in the declaration of a British protectorate in 1894; a Special Commissioner was appointed from Britain to administer the protectorate.

In 1895 what is now the Republic of Kenya became the East African Protectorate,[32] under the charge of the Consul General at Zanzibar. This arrangement would seem to suggest that the British regarded this territory as still relatively insignificant. Through the 1870s and 1880s this area had been only a highway for missionaries, explorers and company personnel travelling to the Great Lakes and the kingdom of Buganda.

The annexation of Kenya and the Arab coast by the British placed the work of the British Protestant missions on a permanent basis all over the area. They could now launch their campaign against slavery successfully. With their stations now in a British protectorate, the Protestant missions could confidently expand into untapped areas in the highlands with the full protection of the British government. In 1896 the British government began the construction of the Kenya-Uganda railway which, among other things, was to speed up and facilitate occupation of the Kenya highlands by the British missions, among others.

Arthur Hardinge, the new Consul General for Zanzibar and the Commissioner for the East Africa Protectorate, arrived at Mombasa to take over the administration of the protectorate. At an open *baraza* with the Wali of Mombasa and Arab elders, Lloyd Mathews, the first minister at Zanzibar, hastily assured the Arabs that their laws and customs would be respected, thus dispelling the fear that the substitution of British rule for company rule would be immediately followed by the abolition of slavery.[33] But Hardinge was faced with the Arab rebellion on the coast.

In 1895 it was clear that the Arabs on the northern coast would engage in open resistance. Early that year a dispute arose at Takaungu where IBEAC's nominee for the post of Wali, upon the death of the incumbent, Salim bin Hamis, was unacceptable to the majority of the Mazrui. Mbaruk bin Rashid, a nephew of the Wali of Gazi, claimed he had a legal right to succeed according to Muslim law. However, when Hardinge took over in 1895 the dispute developed into an open rebellion of the Mazrui, led by Mbaruk of Gazi, against the British. Mbaruk held considerable power over the coast; his authority extended from Umba to Mombasa, and his influence in the interior was paramount over the Wadigo and the Wanduruma.[34]

The Arabs' first attack was naturally directed at the mission stations. Almost all the missions suffered several attacks and houses and property were destroyed. Rabai was twice attacked.[35] These stations were tangible symbols of the alien rule, and the campaign against the Arab religion and social structure which the missionaries had conducted led to their being the first targets of attack.

In the struggle, however, the succession issue overshadowed the major issue of religion and slavery which would certainly have rallied the support of the majority of coastal Arabs with far greater results than the government would have been able to contain. In this issue of the succession to Takaungu, the Arabs were divided into two camps and there was, therefore, no such strong rallying force. Hardinge reported that it was fortunate that the quarrel arose out of a mere political question rather than resistance of the abolition of slavery which would have united them all against the Europeans because it would have given a religious import to the movement.[36] Consequently the Mazrui Arabs were defeated, with the help of troops from India.

About the same time that the Commissioner was engaged in the hostilities between the British and the Arabs for supremacy of the coast, the missionaries, with the CMS in the lead, addressed themselves to the question of slavery. In England the missionaries had a powerful mouthpiece to speak for abolition in the British and Foreign Anti-Slavery Society which was reformed out of the Anti-Slavery Society after the Emancipation Act of 1833. The Anti-Slavery Society was committed to the total abolition of slavery in the British Empire, and began to campaign in England for the abolition of slavery in Zanzibar after 1890 when, under the Anglo-German Treaty, Zanzibar became a British protectorate and hence part of the British Empire. The Brussels Act, signed by the European powers with interests in Africa, added more strength to the society's struggle for abolition, for it made it obligatory for Great Britain to abolish slavery in Zanzibar and in British territories.

In 1895 the case for the abolition of slavery in the coastal area of the East African Protectorate was even stronger than for Zanzibar. The coast, which had hitherto been leased to IBEAC by the Sultan, formed part of the protectorate and hence of the British Empire. Afred Tucker was quick to point out to the British authorities in East Africa and London that unlike Zanzibar, where the Sultan held the executive power, the British government, through the Commissioner, held the executive power on the Mombasa coast.[37] There was therefore no question of postponing immediate abolition on the coast since it was already illegal for slavery to exist in a British-administered territory. He wrote:

the question of immediate abolition is more or less one of finance and energetic government ... Knowing what I do of the traffic of upcountry and slave life at the coast I earnestly hope that no considerations of the expenses involved or the labour entailed will be allowed to interfere ... with the adoption of a policy so righteous in itself and which is to be of beneficial results.[38]

As for Zanzibar, the missionaries and the Anti-Slavery Society argued that abolition should have been effected five years before when Zanzibar became a British protectorate. Slavery in Zanzibar, they argued, had existed illegally for five years. But on this issue the British representatives at Zanzibar were not agreed. They argued, in economic terms, against abrupt abolition. They held the view that wholesale and immediate abolition would ruin the economy of the islands and would bankrupt the Arab plantation owners. They preferred perpetuating slavery until it died a natural death, to strangling the whole economy of the islands and the coast by advocating abrupt abolition. Gerald Portal summed up the feeling of the British consulate at Zanzibar in 1889:

It is admitted by everyone who has had personal acquaintance and experience of the social conditions of this country ... that any measure involving a sudden and complete cessation of this system of slavery and the wholesale liberation of all existing slaves, would be calculated to cause social revolution, entailing absolute ruin on hundreds of Arab land owners and proprietors to an extent that would neither be politic nor justified.[39]

The British government, which was committed to a minimum of expenditure in overseas territories, was more apt to support the view of their representatives at Zanzibar than those expressed by the missionaries as long as such a policy involved the British government in very little expenditure.

Lord Kimberley, the Foreign Secretary, had instructed Hardinge in his appointment merely to:

insist on the faithful execution of the measures which have already been resolved upon for the purpose of the gradual abolition of slavery in the Sultan's Dominions and to recommend any further measures which might seem to you feasible for facilitating and accelerating this object without injustice to the Mohamedan owners.[40]

These instructions fell far short of the expectations of the missionaries and abolitionists who wanted immediate abolition.

The measures against slavery that Hardinge was to insist upon had been passed by Seyyid Ali in August 1890,[41] but they were made void by the Sultan's proclamation, in agreement with Consul Euan Smith, made almost immediately afterwards owing to fear of rebellion by the Arabs against the original decree. The decree was most revolutionary for the Arab landowners, and had it been enforced would have had far-reaching results. The decree forbade all transactions in slaves; the slaves of a master who died leaving no heir were to be freed and the houses of slave brokers were to be closed forthwith. Any slave owner who treated his slaves cruelly was to be brought before the courts and punished, and those who punished their slaves excessively and inhumanely were to forfeit their right to own slaves. Slaves could not accuse their masters of cruelty before the Kadhis. British Indian subjects who had previously evaded the law by practising in the name of their Arab or Swahili wives could no longer do so. The decree extended its area of operation to freed slaves, some of whom themselves employed slaves. Most important of all, slaves could now purchase their freedom at a fair and reasonable price.[42] As a result of the decree Arab ill-feeling was widespread in Zanzibar and Pemba, and rumours were current in Zanzibar that the Arabs were planning to sabotage the treaty and create chaos by murdering the Sultan and the British Consul, Euan Smith. There were even greater fears that the slaves, jubilant over the new decree, would take the law into their own hands and rise up against their masters.[43] The voice of the Arab cause and consequently those who wanted to perpetuate the exploitation of one class by another, for economic reasons, triumphed in August when Euan Smith advised a countermeasure to give the Arabs control of their slaves. The Sultan issued two proclamations: the first made it illegal for slaves to run away and the second ruled that slave owners were not obliged to sell their freedom to those slaves who requested it.[44] Thus the slaves were in no better a position than they were before the decree was passed; they could not buy their freedom, nor could they run away and seek refuge in the mission stations. On this last point the Foreign Office was very emphatic. It declared that the missionaries had no legal right to give refuge to slaves, and that when they did so in extreme cases of peril and on humanitarian grounds it was at their own risk.[45]

The anti-slavery policy that Hardinge was required by the Foreign Office to pursue was therefore meaningless and was at best aimed only at ameliorating the conditions of the slaves. There was to be emancipation but on the basis of justice and full benefits to the slave owners. Moreover it was to come in the distant future when the government was to substitute for slave labour the labour of free men, particularly Indian coolies, efficient and regular enough to sustain the wealth of the Arabs and to keep the economy of the islands going. These conditions were in full accord with Hardinge's ideas.

But in 1895 the Anti-Slavery Society and the missionaries stepped up their campaign for abolition. Their representatives, among them J. A. Pearse, a Quaker and ardent advocate of immediate abolition, raised the question in Parliament.[46] Backed by strong public opinion the British House of Commons approved immediate abolition in principle. Lord Kimberley telegraphed Hardinge the following morning to expedite his recommendations for abolition. He further stated that the British government was willing to make up for 'the deficit in loss of revenue with a grant from the British Treasury.'[47]

However, Hardinge was the greatest protagonist of the Arab slave-owning class and as Consulate General and Commissioner for Zanzibar and the East African Protectorate, he consequently pressed for the maintenance of the status quo in the islands and on the mainland. Hardinge had served in the Middle East from 1886–94:[48] there he had come into contact with the Arabs and studied with admiration and enthusiasm their culture, customs, laws, religion and politics. It was in the Middle East that his sympathy with Islam and its social structure was formed as he discovered that slavery was bound up with the whole Arab social structure. For example, he was convinced that it was difficult to talk of the abolition of slavery without the larger question of the destruction of the whole Arab social structure. The admiration he bore for the Arabs and their social structure therefore determined the policy that he pursued when he was transferred to East Africa in 1894.

Hardinge's argument against immediate abolition in Zanzibar revolved around the question of the economic ruin such a step would bring. He pointed out that such a step would ruin the clove industry which was the backbone of the island's economy. He estimated that the sultanate would be faced with a deficit of £35 000 a year,[49] a figure which was likely to persuade the Foreign Office to compromise public opinion and adopt a policy of gradual abolition so as to minimise the burden on the British Treasury. However the Anti-Slavery movement stepped up its pressure, appointing a representative, Donald Mackenzie, to gather evidence. Mackenzie pointed out that immediate abolition would not entail the economic ruin of the country as 'the freed slaves would still have to work for their living and if they were paid adequate wages ... they would work much better.'[50]

Lord Salisbury, who took over from the Liberals in June 1895, accepted Hardinge's proposal, notwithstanding public pressure, that emancipation should be a gradual process, that the Arabs should be fairly compensated, and that concubines who, Hardinge had argued, became wives once they had children by their masters, were not to be affected by the decree. In April 1897 the Sultan signed the law putting an end to the legal status of slavery

Freetown Mission School, 1875

Slaves in Chains

in Zanzibar and Pemba. Henceforth the machinery to effect gradual emancipation was instituted.

The 1897 Act did not cover the mainland coast of the East African Protectorate, for Hardinge had succeeded in persuading the Foreign Office to postpone it. If abolition was to come, it was certainly in the best interests of the Arabs as a whole that it should not come at the same time on both the mainland and the islands. Hardinge had seized the opportunity of the Mazrui rebellion of 1895–1896 to press that the abolition of slavery on the mainland coast must be postponed to the distant future, until the coast was pacified. Early in 1896, fearing that the missionaries and the Anti-Slavery Society were swinging public opinion to immediate abolition, he telegraphed the Foreign Office requesting that 'no measure against slavery may be imposed till the coast [is] pacified. Elders of Mombasa and Malindi have expressed their dissatisfaction with the operation of the recent laws against slavery.'[51]

Early in 1895 when Tucker took up the case for abolition on the mainland, Hardinge maintained that it would have far more serious effects there than on the islands and was likely to meet with

open armed resistance in so far as besides the Arab chiefs there were beyond the ten mile strip large colonies of runaway slaves, who themselves are slave owners and live by stealing or decoying slaves away from the coast.[52]

The request for postponement until he had pacified the coast received approval from the Foreign Office.

Meanwhile Hardinge, much to the regret of the Protestant missions, painted as good a picture as he could of the conditions of the slaves on the mainland, to persuade the Foreign Office and public opinion in England that slavery there differed greatly from that in Zanzibar and even more from that which had been carried on on the American and West Indian plantations. Hardinge put forward the thesis that the kind of slavery on the mainland coast was rural slavery, more comparable to the *metayer* system in France than to other slave systems.[53] Here the Arabs owned large estates of coconuts, corn and cassava worked by slave labour, but, he argued, the Arabs were absentee landlords, living in the coastal towns of Mombasa, Malindi, Lamu and

c

Vanga. Thus the slaves were left much to themselves as small farmers who, in return for their right to cultivate the owner's land, paid a share of the harvest in rent. Their local affairs were in the hands of their own village elders or headmen. Such an argument carried weight with outside observers and to the British Foreign Office, which was committed to retrenchment overseas.

At about the same time Tucker took a test case to the court at Mombasa to prove that a majority of the slaves on the mainland were illegally held by the Arabs.[54] Following upon the Act of 1873 that brought an end to the East African slave trade, the Sultan of Zanzibar, Seyyid Barghash, issued a proclamation in 1876 to put into force the terms of the Act in his East African dominions. Under the proclamation slave-trading was henceforth declared illegal as was the importation of slaves from the interior. Tucker brought before the Provincial Court at Mombasa the case of Kheri Karibu who, he alleged, had been enslaved and held illegally since she had been brought from the mainland at some time after 1876. The Arab assessors found the case proven and declared that Kheri Karibu should be freed.[55] The implication of the decision was that every slave who had been brought from upcountry since April 1876 was held illegally. The bishop estimated that the slaves affected by the pronouncement formed three-quarters of all those then living in Mombasa and the coastal area. But above all the court ruling invalidated the argument that emancipation would cost the British government a great deal in compensatory payments to the Arabs, for compensation would now have to be paid only for a quarter of the slave population on the mainland coast: the majority would be emancipated without any financial obligation to the Arabs since they were held illegally. Tucker said

the far reaching character of this decision was little realised by the Mohammedan assessors to whose interpretation of the decree the judgement was due or I hardly think they would have ventured to identify themselves with such a pronouncement. Its bearing on the abolition was very close [for] it reduced almost to vanishing point the amount that would be due in way of compensation.[56]

Hardinge, however, did not give up the battle for the Arab

landed aristocracy on the mainland. He knew abolition would come, but first he wanted to curb the power of the missions and ensure that the Arab plantation owners would get the labour they needed when abolition came. He therefore proposed that abolition should be followed by corvée (compulsory labour for part of the year), the taxation of freed slaves and emigration laws,[57] devices all directed at safeguarding the prosperity of the Arab estates through the labour of people theoretically emancipated but the freed slaves still effectively enslaved.

Hardinge also took steps against the missions. Since 1874 the missionary in charge of Rabai had been recognised as the civil authority for the subdistrict. Both IBEAC and the colonial government had respected this arrangement, but Hardinge was not prepared to do so. Maintaining that he wanted uniformity in the local administration of the coast, he placed Rabai under the jurisdiction of the Wilayet of Mombasa[58] and appointed Ali bin Sultan as assistant to the Wali of Mombasa 'with immediate jurisdiction over the whole Wilayet outside the island [of Mombasa] and substituting him for the missionary in charge as the chief local authority in Rabai.'[59]

The Foreign Office overruled him in this, as it did over proposals that every runaway slave should be compelled to compensate his Arab master.[60] George Curzon, Under-Secretary of State at the Foreign Office, maintained that such a step was designed exclusively in the interests of the slave owners and, as such, would be bitterly opposed by the missionaries, and attacked in the British Parliament. He could not agree that the CMS should be deprived of privileges it had enjoyed for many years. Curzon, irritated by what he called Hardinge's pro-slavery feelings and his conflict with Tucker, reported:

He [Hardinge] has made a series of proposals all of which we have had to veto and which have ... attempted to strain proclamation, regulations and edicts rather unfairly in the interests of the system which he supports but which the House of Commons will not have. None of these successive proposals of his will bear the light of official publication.[61]

The CMS was not deterred by the hostile attitude adopted by Hardinge. With the support of the Foreign Office the battle the missions were waging for the abolition of slavery seemed almost won. In 1898, a month after the Foreign Office overruled Hardinge's proposal that runaway slaves should be forced to compensate their masters, the CMS committee in England addressed a memorandum to Lord Salisbury, the Prime Minister, calling for the immediate abolition of slavery in the British East African Protectorate.[62]

Both Tucker and Hardinge left the East African Protectorate while the battle for abolition was still on. When the East Africa Mission was divided into two Tucker left to take over the diocese of Uganda, where he continued to campaign for the abolition of slavery. Hardinge's departure a few months later, in 1900, marked the end of the supremacy of Arab interests on the coast. Tucker hailed Hardinge's transfer to Persia as the dismissal he had pressed for, while Hardinge greeted that of Bishop Tucker with equal exultation.[63]

William George Peel, the new bishop of the diocese of Mombasa, carried Tucker's banner with equal vigour and dedication. In 1907 the long-awaited abolition of slavery on the coast of Kenya was finally achieved. The Foreign Office agreed to compensate the Arabs for the loss of their slaves and courts for this purpose were set up in all the big coastal towns in 1910.[64] The following year was the last opportunity for the Arabs on the mainland and in Zanzibar to claim compensation. In 1919 Charles Hobley reported that the number of slaves liberated from October 1, 1907 to April 30, 1916 was 7 683 and the total amount of compensation given to the Arabs for the same period was 449 757.55 rupees.[65]

The abolition of slavery in Kenya marked the successful end of a battle which the missionaries had been waging since 1874. The missionaries could well congratulate themselves on achieving one of the major objectives bequeathed to them by Livingstone. The missionaries, undeterred by slavery, could now embark upon the evangelisation of the interior of Kenya, a task that had already begun around the turn of the century.

NOTES

1. Roland Oliver and Gervase Mathew (eds.), *History of East Africa*, Vol. I (Oxford, 1963), pp. 382–385; map p. 374.
2. Frere to Granville, March 10, 1873 and April 5, 1873, FO 84/1390 and FO 84/1390, PRO.

3. Reginald Coupland, *The Exploitation of East Africa 1856–1900: The Slave Trade and the Scramble* (London, 1939), pp. 251–252.
4. Hardinge to Lord Salisbury, April 12, 1896, FO 107/51.
5. Oliver and Mathew, *History of East Africa*, pp. 378–381.
6. *Ibid.*, p. 386.
7. Hardinge to Lord Salisbury, April 12, 1896, FO 107/51, PRO.
8. *Ibid.*
9. Euan Smith to Lord Salisbury, January 11, 1889, FO 84/1975, PRO.
10. William Mackenzie, 'Circular Letter to all Mission Stations,' January 5, 1889, in Euan Smith to Lord Salisbury, January 11, 1889, FO 84/1975, PRO.
11. *Church Missionary Intelligencer*, 1893, p. 3.
12. C. W. Hobley, *Kenya from Chartered Company to Crown Colony* (London, 1905), pp. 32–33.
13. *Church Missionary Intelligencer*, 1893, p. 3.
14. Hardinge to Lord Salisbury, April 12, 1896, FO 107/51, PRO.
15. Alfred Tucker, *Eighteen Years in Uganda and East Africa*, 2nd ed. (London, 1911), Vol. II, p. 62.
16. Hardinge to Lord Salisbury, April 12, 1896, FO 107/51, PRO.
17. Alfred Tucker to Lang, June 11, 1890, G3 A5/06, CMS Archives, London.
18. Mary Evelyn Townsend, *The Rise and Fall of Germany's Colonial Empire 1884–1919* (New York, 1930), pp. 131–141.
19. *Ibid.*
20. Taylor to Price, August 17, 1888, G3 A5/05, CMS Archives, London.
21. Steggal to Keith Anstrunther, September 23, 1890, in Euan Smith to Lord Salisbury, November 24, 1890, FO 84/2066, PRO.
22. *Ibid.*
23. William S. Price, *My Third Campaign in East Africa* (London, 1890), pp. 140–141.
24. Cathleen Stahl, *History of the Chagga People of Kilimanjaro* (London, 1964), p. 255.
25. *Church Missionary Intelligencer*, 1893, p. 248.
26. Interview with Petro I. Marealle, February 2 and 4, 1966.
27. Interview with Marealle, February 2 and 4, 1966 and communication from Marealle, April 5, 1966. Interview with Joseph Mawalla, June 10, 1966.
28. Tucker to Portal, June 19, 1892, in Portal to Lord Salisbury, June 30, 1892, FO 84/2231, PRO. Steggal to Lang, June 22, 1892, G3 A5/08, CMS Archives, London.
29. Steggal to Lang, July 30, 1892, G3 A5/08, CMS Archives, London.
30. *Ibid.* Also interview with Petro Merinyo, June 20 and 24, 1966.
31. Stahl, pp. 264–265.
32. *Ibid.*, p. 389.
33. L. W. Hollingsworth, *Zanzibar under the Foreign Office, 1890–1913* (London, 1953), p. 107.
34. Hardinge to Lord Salisbury, April 22, 1896, FO 107/51, PRO.
35. Hardinge to Lord Salisbury, July 6, 1895, FO 107/36, PRO.

36. Hardinge to Lord Salisbury, April 12, 1896, FO 107/51, PRO.
37. Tucker, I, p. 66.
38. *Ibid.*
39. Portal to Lord Salisbury, September 23, 1889, FO 84/1980, PRO.
40. Kimberley to Hardinge, May 5, 1894, FO 107/16 PRO.
41. Euan Smith to Lord Salisbury, August 3, 1890, FO 84/2063, PRO.
42. Hollingsworth, Appendix I, pp. 217–219.
43. *Ibid.*, p. 54.
44. *Ibid.*
45. Salisbury to Euan Smith, February 1, 1889, FO 84/1973, PRO.
46. *Ibid.*, p. 136.
47. Kimberley to Hardinge, March 9, 1895, FO 107/40 (telegram), PRO.
48. Arthur Hardinge, *A Diplomatist in the East* (London, 1928), pp. 246–250.
49. Hardinge to Kimberley, March 13, 1895, FO 107/35, PRO.
50. Hollingsworth, p. 139.
51. Hardinge to Lord Salisbury, January 19, 1896, FO 107/49, PRO.
52. Hardinge to Kimberley, June 24, 1895, FO 107/36, PRO.
53. Hardinge to Kimberley, June 24, 1895, FO 107/36, PRO.
54. Tucker, II, p. 103.
55. *Ibid.*
56. *Ibid.*
57. Hardinge to Kimberley, June 24, 1895, FO 403/36, PRO.
58. Hardinge to Lord Salisbury, August 24, 1897, FO 107/79, PRO.
59. *Ibid.*
60. Salisbury to Hardinge, February 23, 1898, FO 107/92, PRO.
61. Curzon to Salisbury (Minute), May 9, 1898, FO 107/92, PRO.
62. Fox to Lord Salisbury, April 30, 1898, G3 A5/L8, CMS Archives, London.
63. Hardinge to Lord Salisbury, February 9, 1899, FO 2/189.
64. Hollingsworth, p. 158.
65. Hobley to the Chief Secretary, Nairobi, February 5, 1919, Coast 47/1123, Nairobi Archives.

4

The Liberated Africans on the Mombasa Coast, 1874-1904

In 1874, the year after the abolition of the East African slave trade, the CMS established Freretown colony, the first Freretown settlers were repatriates from India; the majority came from Bombay, whence the popular appellation, Bombay Africans. More than a hundred and fifty returned from Bombay to settle in Freretown in 1875. They were some of the slaves whom British naval cruisers patrolling the Indian Ocean rescued from Arab dhows and made over to India, then a British possession where slave trade had been illegal since 1807. The first group was sent to India in 1847. At first the British India Government used to distribute them indiscriminately, some to Muslim, Hindu and European families, while others were set at liberty.[1]

This indiscriminate distribution rarely led to any real freedom for the penniless exiles. The government would have liked to give them into the care of the missions, but feared that to do so would alienate the preponderantly Muslim population in India. Missionaries resident in Bombay took considerable pains to point out that the freed slaves would not attain real freedom until they had acquired skills which would make them self-supporting. Hoping that most of the freed slaves would finally return to East Africa once the slave trade was abolished, they urged that in the meantime colonies should be established where the freed slaves could live secure and at liberty. The government, conscious of these problems, initiated a training programme which would provide them with the skills they needed to support themselves in India.

In 1855 W. S. Price established the Christian village of Sharanpur, near Nasik, where industrial training was given, and in 1860 most of the liberated African slaves were settled here to be trained in Christianity and taught various trades with the help of a subsidy from the government. Price sums up the mission's policy on the freed slaves as follows:

> viewing it as a providential opening, and hoping that ... some of those placed under care might eventually become Evangelists in their country, I consented to the proposal of the Government; some twenty-five or thirty boys and girls already in Bombay were at once transferred to Sharanpur, and thus the African Asylum had its beginning ... They came to us in batches varying from twenty to fifty in number, and as to age, ranging from children of six to young men and young women of eighteen or twenty.[2]

The government also began to give some industrial training at its own farm at Pachora. While we know of the numbers of those who passed through the CMS—there were over two hundred —and who finally returned to Freretown, the number of those who passed through Pachora is still to be established when more research into the activities of the British Government in India is done. We know however, that among those who returned to East Africa in 1875, most came from Nasik and only a few from Pachora.

At Nasik the freed slaves were first trained as Christians. But to make them and their families self-supporting, the CMS also gave them training in industrial skills. While some were trained as catechists, evangelists and teachers, others were trained as carpenters, masons and bricklayers; the women were taught needlework and weaving.

The CMS quickly made progress in their task of training the ex-slaves. In 1869 William Salt Price happily reported that 'five lads had passed the Normal entrance examination and [the CMS] that some of them would matriculate at Bombay University and become School masters, either in India or in their native country.[3] Three years earlier he had not anticipated so great a progress would be attained so quickly with freed slaves, and hailed their coming to the Asylum as a God-sent blessing to the mission. He wrote:

It seemed in a way not thought of by us it pleased God to give the CMS a chief share in the work of carrying the Gospel to East Africa as well as to West Africa thus adding fresh significance to the designation which is given to the society.[4]

Before their final return there, some of them had made a considerable contribution to East Africa. In 1865 nine of them had accompanied Dr David Livingstone to East and Central Africa where their role as interpreters and negotiators helped him to gain a better knowledge of the interior. Johannes Rebmann had also sent two families to be chief catechists at Rabai. Without the efforts of George David as a catechist, the work of the CMS at Rabai between 1841 and 1874 would have collapsed. It was George David who told Frere that provided the mission concentrated more on industrial training, in contrast to the abstract 'ascetic life of self-denial and indifference to all worldly enjoyments and employment'[5] which Rebmann had so unsuccessfully taught the Nyika, there would be a break-through in the work of the mission to the people around. Teaching the Africans skills to make them self-supporting, George David maintained, would make the lives of the Christians meaningful and so attract them towards Christianity, while that emphasised by Rebmann only aroused their admiration without converting them.

Around 1873 some of the Bombay Africans—Mathew Wellington, Jacob Wainwright, William Benjamin, Kalos and Legget, left Nasik to accompany Stanley in his search for Livingstone, never to return to Bombay. In 1874 Mathew Wellington left Zanzibar for Freretown to become one of the first pioneers of the settlement; we are told he assisted Price in transforming the jungle into a happy settlement as he did in the training of the freed slaves there. Jacob Wainwright, a dresser, and Kalos lived and died in Zanzibar; Legget and William Benjamin returned to their home in Mozambique where they also became missionaries to their own people; the former died in 1906 and the latter in 1915.

Inevitably, the first African readers, teachers, catechists and pastors were all freed slaves. Nasik in Bombay was started with the purpose of turning out evangelists and teachers and the first thing that William Price, the first superintendent of Freretown settlement, did was to establish a school for children and adults. While the children learned the alphabet, the adults were taught to read the Bible. A great step forward was taken in 1888 when a Divinity School for the training of evangelists and teachers for all CMS stations was begun at Freretown. William Price hailed it a very significant day for the history of the East African Mission. He wrote:

We took the first steps in the formation of a training class for promising young men as teachers and evangelists. We begin with a modest number of nine and Fitch is the first Principal.[6]

Freretown henceforth became a training school for all the future teachers, readers, evangelists and pastors of the CMS Mission in East Africa. The UMCA had taken similar steps in 1875 when it started Kiungani school in Zanzibar for the training of all the workers of the UMCA mission in East and Central Africa. Pupils for both schools were selected from all their stations; the CMS drew pupils from as far afield as Central Tanganyika, Moshi and the Mombasa hinterland; the UMCA from its mission stations in Southern Tanganyika and Malawi as well as in Zanzibar and Magila.

It may be said that for the whole of the transitional period, a period extending for over fifty years on the coast and up to the end of the First World War for the interior of Kenya, the story of the church, its successes and failures, is indeed the story of the early African catechists, readers and pastors. For the Mombasa coast particularly during the period 1874–1904, the initiative came from the Bombay Africans and they held the leadership for a generation before they were joined by some of the newly freed slaves. They were cut out for leadership by their education and experience. First they were literate in English, Gujerati, Swahili and in their own vernaculars; Swahili and English was a great use to their work on the coast. They were also qualified as artisans, small traders and agriculturalists, attributes which the Victorian missions both valued and respected. Some of them had also held important jobs in the Indian Railways and in the Public Works Department in Bombay.

The first duty of the Bombay Africans centred on the central stations of Freretown and Rabai where, when there was a Euro-

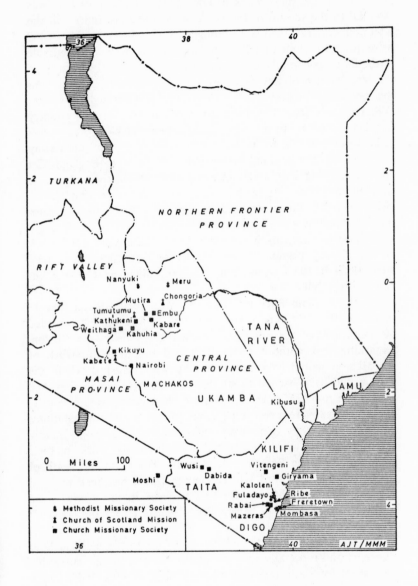

Sketch map showing British Mission stations in Kenya east
of the rift valley

pean in charge they worked under him. Their presence was essential to the success of the work of the missions. Indeed all the white missionaries who were brought to the mission at this period were quick to admit that the Bombay Africans were indispensable in the East African Mission, and they protested vehemently against the transference of any of them from the central stations. Thus the Rev. Lamb protested when William Price proposed to transfer William Jones from Freretown for work in the Giriama country in 1876. 'It seems to me to be folly when the work has almost to be begun here,' he wrote, 'to talk of sending William Jones away —if you do that we had better return at once to England. Get one work going here and find a suitable person, then of course Giriama and other places too shall have due attention.'[7] Similarly when Mr Binns reported in 1876 that the male congregation at Rabai was well cared for by George David he strongly advised against moving him as this would disturb the good work he had already begun. Except on very few occasions these men were alone in the stations, not only preaching and teaching but also settling civil cases.

In 1882 William Price was in East Africa for a second time to report on the prospects of the East African Mission. He recorded his assessment of the role of the Bombay Africans in the Mission, remarking that without their effort and initiative the work of the Mission would have failed. It may well be asked where the CMS would have been without the valuable help which they had given. The number of the freed slaves had grown tremendously: by 1880 there were 3 000 freed slaves in the two mission stations, while in 1874–1875 there were only 200. All these were mainly cared for, taught the Bible and trained in industrial work for their self-support by the Bombay Africans. In 1884 upon the death of George David, Handford wrote: 'George David has been engaged in the work of the Mission for twenty years in this country and his place cannot possibly be supplied. What to do for the flock left without a shepherd I know not.'[8]

The Bombay African travelled from place to place throughout the coast and especially throughout the Nyika country, surveying new areas for the establishment of mission stations. Indeed they were responsible for the establishment of new stations in the area. From the very beginning both George David and William Jones extended their preaching beyond the borders of Freretown and

Rabai. We are told that William Jones together with Samuel Isenberg, another catechist of Buni Hill, preached to the Kaya nearby in 1875. Even as early as this he could happily report some results however disillusioned he might have been: 'The Wanika of Dr Krapf's time are not the Wanika of the present day. The Wanika of the present day hear the word of God most gladly and indeed I am of the opinion that the time has truly come when the Wanika should be won to Christ.'[9]

In 1875 George David visited Godoma and preached to the Giriama. Their response was good: they agreed to send their children to Rabai for schooling and further requested a teacher of religion to be stationed at Godoma. 'If they fulfil their promise, he wrote, 'we shall have eight children from Godoma under instruction at Rabai. These men do this in order that they may have teachers they have long been asking Mr Rebmann for but got none ... I hope the plan is from the Lord and that it will succeed so that in course of time from the primeval forests of Godoma songs of praise may be raised to him.[10] David also surveyed another town, Jilore, fifteen miles from Malindi and about seventy miles from Mombasa, in Giriama—and found it most suitable for a mission station. 'From here,' David wrote, 'the gospel could easily be conveyed to the Wakamba in the interior.'[11] The CMS did eventually establish a station there in 1890.

In 1878 William Jones, the other important catechist who was ordained Deacon in 1885 and Archdeacon in 1896, went on a two weeks' marathon tour to the Duruma, another section of the Nyika. At Mazota, presumably then the capital of the Duruma, he preached to the people. About Mazota he wrote, 'it was at one time a famous place but it is now deserted.' At Kaya Mvuvuni which William Jones and his party reached on August 10, Jones 'was amply paid for his labour by the people's earnestness and attentiveness to all that was spoken to them about the kingdom of heaven.'[12] At Chamamba, another village, his journal August 13 recorded:

This day at an early hour many people around Chamamba district came to see the black Mzungu with Chuo. The news reached many of them last night for as soon as I arrived as many as I could find in the village of Mwandani I summoned them to come forth to hear the word of God. How willingly they came after I sent for them. They were more attached to me when I showed them the drawings of some of the illustrated London News ... I then kept the papers and ... told them how infinitely low in the scales of civilisation we Africans as a nation were in comparison with our brethren Europeans, Asiatics and Americans.[13]

Again in 1880 William Jones was responsible for making it possible for the CMS to start work among the Taita. After Wray and Morris, both white missionaries, had tried for two years in vain to overcome the hostility and the opposition of Taita leaders to mission work in their country, William Price sent William Jones to resolve the problem. Price chose him as a last resort because he said:

he [William Jones] knows many of them well and is known and respected by them; besides he is a man of tact and as a native he can reason with them more than us. If any one can bring these poor misguided people to their senses it is him.[14]

It was only after he had visited Taita and talked to the elders that Morris happily reported that the people 'had had the opportunity of expressing their feelings. Jones had seen many of them and talked to them. We had permission to move freely over the greater part of the mountain [Taita Hills].[15]

Much the same story can be told of the achievements of the first catechists of the UMCA. For example, Charles Sulleiman, a freed slave and a Kiungani graduate but one of the first readers at Masasi, was responsible for carrying the gospel to the villages around Masasi in 1881. But perhaps more significant was that he chose to remain in Masasi to carry on the gospel in 1883 after the Gwangara raid on the mission in 1882. All the other freed slaves left for either the new station in Newala or Zanzibar. Charles Sulleiman remained to preach to the people around and he was able to keep the gospel alive in an area which was almost abandoned.

Not many mission stations were established on the coast. Only three major stations, Jilore, Taita, Shimba Hill, besides Rabai and Freetown and several sub-stations, were established. Outside the Mombasa coast there were also established mission stations at

Moshi, Mamboia and Mpwapwa in Tanganyika. Nonetheless the Bombay Africans had preached to the villagers in many parts of the coast and made them at least aware of their presence. Although not many converts were won, the journeys they made which covered the whole of the coast were significant landmarks in its history. The enthusiasm and vigour with which they preached to the coastal societies was unequalled and perhaps comparable only with that of the evangelists working in England about the same time: Kenneth MacDougal, District Officer at Rabai, remarked caustically in 1911:

The native Christian adherents number 700–800 but only a minority of these are Rabai and Wagirama. The majority are resident aliens, many of the *Watoro*, have gathered round the Mission and settled at Rabai. Numbers of these were baptised by William Jones who was at one time in charge of Rabai, with what is admitted by the Missionaries to have been great excess zeal, since most of them were very far from having attained the knowledge of religious matters and the manner of life befitting Christians.[16]

Of remarkable interest was their serious concern about the Christianisation of the African societies on the coast, particularly the Nyika. More broadly perhaps this concern reflects their own appreciation of Western culture and Christianity and the extent to which they were prepared to substitute it for their own. In particular the concern of the Bombay Africans to spread Christianity and Western civilisation to the Nyika runs through the whole period. in 1878 William Jones blamed the CMS for its failure to gain any converts from the Nyika. This he believed lay in the unsystematic approach that the CMS had adopted towards the evangelisation of the Nyika. 'For some years past', he wrote, 'there has been nothing but the coming in and the going out of missionaries and almost all of them are compelled to retreat to England before they are able to do anything for the Africans, much less for Rabai and Kisulutini (Freretown).[17]

In 1904 after the CMS had begun to shift its emphasis from the Mombasa coast to the heavily populated highlands of Kenya, to begin work with the Kikuyu and the Akamba, William Jones expressed even deeper disappointment with his mission for having failed to spread Christianity among the Nyika. By this time the freed slaves as a class were fast disappearing from the Kenya scene; most of them had moved into the interior and into the coastal towns and fused with other Africans. To be sure, William Jones was also lamenting his own failure to spread Christianity to the Nyika, among whom he had worked all his life. In 1904, the year he died, William Jones wrote:

> For nearly half a century, my Lord, what has the Mission done for the Wanyika people from Digo to Giriama country? All these years have been spent upon Rabai and Freretown. Why not raise new stations between Mwaemba and Jilore? By nature Malindi has no signpost, even of the CMS. Kauma on the top of Takaungu, Chonyi, Jabane, Kamoe have all been tantalised from time immemorial with no good results. For half a century the result is some station in the Shimba Hill where Mr Binns is now with not a single convert.[18]

The expansion of the church and of Christianity on the coast before the end of the First World war and long after, albeit a modest record, was undertaken by the Bombay Africans and those whom they trained—also freed slaves. While one must acknowledge the presence of the European missionaries, their background and language problems made their role in the expansion of the historic church vis-à-vis that of the Africans insignificant. Climate alone immobilised many of the white missionaries for many months. There were hardly more than five at any one moment for the CMS spheres in Kenya and Tanzania, and very often not more than one missionary was physically fit to undertake any missionary work of any significance up to at least 1900. No direct contact between the European missionaries and the African societies was possible during this period as African societies opposed the intrusion of European missionaries and of the introduction of Christianity. It is important to remember that this opposition to Christianity from the African population was general throughout East Africa at this period. Then the only means of contact and of spreading Christianity to the African societies was the African Christians whom the white missionaries had brought with them or whom they had trained in the central stations. This, Dr Iliffe has observed was also true of the Lutheran missionaries in Unyakyusa, of the UMCA in Bondei and Masasi, of the Holy Ghost Fathers in Bagamoyo and the Benedictines. And he confirms: 'Early missionaries probably had less impact on the societies they met than did the African Christians they invariably brought with them, and on whom they greatly depended.[19]

Equally important were the observations they made about the areas through which they passed. Their comments about the political situation on the coast were remarkably accurate. Visiting Giriama, William Jones found that the Masai were dreaded in every village. The Wanyika, in self-defence, were living either on the tops of the hills or down in the deep valleys far away from the easy reach of the Masai, who he said claimed the right of possessing all the cattle in the world. No wonder, said Jones that 'all the East Coast of Africa was in expectation of a mighty deliverer from the easy reach of the Masai, the common foe'.[20] Jones found Mazota, once famous and heavily populated, deserted because of civil war and the Masai. 'Mbaruk, who represents the once powerful Mazrui dynasty,' he wrote, 'is also endeavouring to give the finishing stroke by extracting large sums of money, cattle, goats, slaves . . .'[21]

In 1885 William Jones accompanied Bishop James Hannington on the fateful journey to Uganda during which Hannington was murdered. Jones survived to give in his journal a penetrating account of the country and the people they met on the way. Of the Kikuyu, he said:

The greedy Suahili last time they were here, as they were in great force took advantage of the poor Wakikuyu when they came down to sell their goods, caught them and made slaves of them. The Suahili traders followed this up by attacking the Wakikuyu in the forest homes, killing some and kidnapping others so that there is little wonder if they have lost faith in Suahili caravans.[22]

All the reports that European travellers and missionaries made at this period about the chaos brought by civil wars and by the incessant Masai attacks on the Akamba and the Nyika on the coast, not to mention on the African societies in the interior, have been publicised widely. The credit for this information as well as for the geographical knowledge of the area which they wrote about has been given to these Europeans – missionaries, travellers and adventurers alike. It is absurd that this credit should not at least be shared with the Bombay Africans. The journals, especially, that these Bombay Africans wrote reveal as much penetrating and useful information about the area as their white contemporaries did.

It is difficult to overemphasise the importance of the work of these first African Christians in the expansion of missionary activity. In the 1870s the European missionaries had protested at attempts to remove the Bombay Africans from their stations to new ones—so valuable was their contribution. But from the 1880s the relations between these first African Christians, especially the Bombay Africans, and the white missionaries began to change. In contrast to the earlier development of Christianity in West Africa, European missionaries in East Africa did not allow the Bombay Africans responsibility commensurate with the heavy burdens which they carried. Ultimately friction developed.

From the beginning the policy of the CMS was to work quickly towards self-supporting, self-propagating and self-governing native churches. This policy was advocated by Henry Venn, secretary of the CMS from 1841–1872. By the early sixties this policy had been a success in West Africa and the first African Bishop, Samuel Crowther, a Sierra Leonean, was consecrated Bishop of Niger Diocese in 1864. This was the second Anglican Diocese in West Africa and the largest in the area. By the late seventies however, notwithstanding the CMS's late beginning at Mombasa, there was enough justification for the CMS to speed up the process of African-isation in the church already adopted on the West Coast of Africa.

William Price thought that wherever there was a native con-gregation a native pastor should be ordained to minister to it. He held the view, already accepted at Salisbury Square, that only African pastors and ministers could superintend and propagate the gospel to their own people. At Freretown Rabai George David, William Jones and Ishmael Seimler were qualified in this task.

In 1876 J. A. Lamb from Yoruba country came to superintend the Mombasa mission when Price left. With his West African experience, Lamb took immediate steps towards achieving an African bishop on the East Coast. On his arrival at Freretown, in 1876, he recommended that George David be given deacon's orders,[23] for he was already doing all the work of an ordained minister except for the administration of the sacraments.

With a view to the realisation of the East African bishopric and ministry, Lamb began a Native Pastorate Fund. In its inaugural meeting, August 30, 1876, it was agreed that each candidate for church membership would contribute twopence toward the Native Pastorate Fund. Most of the Bombay Africans undoubtedly looked forward to the day when one of them, perhaps George David, would, like Samuel Crowther on the Niger, lead the church at Mombasa as their first bishop. In addition to this and to prepare the African Christians for responsibility and leadership, Lamb also took the first steps towards the formation of an African Church Council at Mombasa. He reported:

I want as soon as possible to start the system of leaders selecting, one by one, those who seem to be the leading men in the church and giving them a certain responsibility. In this way a Church Council is formed.[24]

However, Lamb's grand ideas were shortlived. The prospects of another Bishop Crowther which he saw in George David, and which he had written about so enthusiastically, vanished, to re-appear only in the 1950s. From about 1879, conflict between the Bombay Africans and the European missionaries began to develop at Freretown. Lamb and Price were replaced by other Europeans. The change of personalities brought to Mombasa Europeans of different tempers. They began to look at Africans as inferior people, even the Bombay Africans whom their predecessors had treated differently because of their education, and because they were above all Christians. There was also at this same time a separation of duties with the establishment of the post of lay superintendent. Towards the end of 1879, until the rift between J. R. Streeter, A. Menzies and schoolmaster Handford on the one hand and the Bombay Africans on the other, there was increasing antagonism between them and the lay superintendent. It is very difficult to learn from his letters to Salisbury Square the cause of this rancour since he, as indeed almost all the other missionaries at this period, were very inconsistent in their views of the Bombay Africans. In 1879, for example, Streeter spoke highly of them, but the following year he described them as slovenly, drunkards, lazy and liars.[25] During this period resident missionaries at Freretown gave no preferential treatment to the Bombay Africans although they recognised the services that George David, William Jones and Ishmael Seimler were giving to the mission. Thomas Smith, we are told, had superintended every hut and the clearing of every piece of ground, yet he had been flogged and imprisoned without any justification. The actions of the missionaries, therefore, drove the Bombay Africans further and further away from them, and increased their consciousness as a class of themselves above the other freed slaves. Certainly their education, setting them apart in a position of privilege in the mission stations, made them conscious of themselves as a class and widened the gap between them and the newly freed slaves in the stations on the one hand and the Africans around them on the other. Despising both, the Bombay Africans found very much to their surprise that they did not fit into the class of the white missionary immediately above theirs.

In 1881 the conflict between the Bombay Africans and the white missionaries came into the open, and the Bombay Africans decided to appeal to Salisbury Square for redress. The immediate cause for the memorandum they issued was a letter in which the Rev. Menzies had reported to Salisbury Square on the mission and which was printed in the *Church Missionary Intelligencer* without the omission of the controversial and offensive references as was usual with such reports. Menzies had asked that such references be omitted before the letter was made available to the general public. In his letter to Henry Wright, Menzies had referred to the Bombay Africans as 'idle and slovenly in their habits and their women spending most of the time in gossiping ... and sleeping ...'[26] The Bombay Africans therefore, found, a cause for bringing to the open the antagonism that the white missionaries, Menzies and the lay superintendent, Streeter, had borne them from the beginning. The Bombay Africans genuinely believed that they were being oppressed and victimised as a class. In a long memorandum to Salisbury Square, carrying the signatures of George David, Jonah Freeman, Tom Smith, Ishmael Seimler, James Ainsworth and Robert Keating, they said:

We, the so-called Bombay Africans ... call the attention of (the CMS), to the subject we have entitled 'The Bombay

Africans' Defence of their Character.' We have long endured with reports, of the European missionaries and teachers you send us. . . .

With the exception of the Reverend William Salt Price who always . . . reports home distinctly and separately of each department . . . describing what was done in each department . . . so that the two pictures, that is, the wheat and the tares growing together, were seen . . . his successors rarely did so which often grieved us . . . But things have come to such a high pitch (we) must speak for ourselves.

The Reverend Menzies wrote in his letter to you that the Bombay Africans are idle and slovenly in their habits, their women spend much of their time gossiping from house to house and sleeping when they should be working. Perhaps you might say this does not include the heads of the place . . . if in describing the Bombay Africans (the missionaries) had not made a distinction between (the heads of the places) and the rest, would any description exclude the heads or other hopeful men and women? It is this (generalisation) which has given all the Bombay Africans a very bad name and a bad certificate throughout the world.

(Regarding the usefulness of the Bombay Africans), when the Reverend Mr and Mrs Lamb left Freretown on March 20, 1877 . . . his work was carried on by Mr Streeter and the Bombay Africans. The Makua and other mixed tribes baptized were first taken in hand by David who began to teach them letters ABC . . . every Friday evening from eight to nine . . . Mr Streeter . . . changed it from nine to morning and freed George David and placed Ishmael not only to teach them letters but texts and to say prayers. At the end of calling their names Mr Ishmael is freed and used as interpreter of cases and Thomas Smith steps in. There is neither a plot of ground which has been cultivated, nor a hut which has been raised on the settlement of which Thomas Smith has not had a hand in.

The School which is conducted by Mr Handford here has four Bombay Africans who daily labour with him willingly. In his absence the school is entirely conducted by them. The Sunday School which is conducted by Mr Streeter has eight teachers, all Bombay Africans. As regards the work departments . . . they are carried by the Bombay Africans. . . .

There are thirty-six Bombay Africans in the Members' Class who hitherto took the Lord's Supper and some of them declined taking the Lord's Supper as planned everywhere in the mission field. Mrs Menzies asked the Bombay African women to help her in her charity work which they did but received no credit. In short, all the work which has been done here and which is being done now by the Europeans, is done through the Bombay Africans. For all this, why would the missionaries be ever murmuring against the Bombay Africans? (Why do they not) leave them and form or begin another station for themselves among the different tribes of the uncivilised Africans without the Bombay Africans? ... It is plain to you from the many letters of your missionaries that the Bombay Africans are the stumbling block of the mission at Mombasa. The Bombay Africans therefore proposed to you that if you want (them) to remain as your people remove them from (Rabai and Freretown) the two stations to another station and give them a God-fearing man as superintendent. If this should be heavy on your part in the way of expenses issue an order for them to leave the places without an exception, and thus the stumbling block will be removed out of the way and everything shall flourish.[27]

At Freretown all the Bombay Africans had been counselling and holding meetings. They had been in a state of near-rebellion for six weeks before they finally wrote the memorandum. 'The catechists and others who wrote the letter, acting as leaders and instigators,' wrote Menzies, 'stirred the rest ... so much so that we had to take very sharp and decided steps to bring them into subjection'.[28] The memorandum is certainly evidence of the ingrowing spirit of independence which, Bishop Peel remarked in 1899, 'was evident in our leading African Christians.'[29] The memorandum was, however, weakened by being submissive couched in the language characteristic of missionaries. The age of the African movement of independence in the church, and of the use of uncompromising language in Kenya, lay in the distant years of the 1920s. It is evident from their memorandum that the Bombay Africans were not seeking independence from the CMS for even when they suggested that they move from the mission station to find another station, they still wanted to remain under the CMS and, consequently, requested that they be given a 'God-fearing superintendent.'[30] Their main concern, therefore, was to seek redress and recognition, and hence their appeal to Salisbury Square for justice and support, rather than outright rebellion from the church. The memorandum antedates many such appeals from African political parties over the heads of the colonial administrator on the spot, to the Colonial Office. The course of action with these early movements was always peaceful. Rebellion, however, came when such appeals failed to produce the hoped-for results.

About the same time began the long and bitter campaign on the Niger Mission, launched by British missionaries to discredit the African clergy and African leadership in their own church. The campaign began about 1880 when European missionaries began to spread reports, without any supporting evidence, on the low morality of the Niger ministry and laity. They directed their charges against the bishopric of Crowther, who had been bishop on the Niger since 1864. In the second half of the decade the campaign had gathered so much force that a number of white missionaries were sent out to the Niger diocese to make allegations that the whole diocese was rife with immorality and corruption, thus proving, that the Africans were not fit to take responsible positions. Widely current in Great Britain at this time were the racist ideas of social Darwinism which proclaimed that Africans were inferior to Anglo-Saxons; these ideas were used to justify imperialism. The leaders of the campaign to purge the Niger Mission of its black bishop and clergy, G. W. Brookes and J. A. Robinson, were racists undoubtedly inspired by social Darwinism.

Events on the East Coast may be said to parallel those of the Niger Mission though in a less dramatic way. In both cases the Europeans became increasingly antagonistic towards the educated Africans for reasons partly connected with their own inferiority and insecurity in the church, and partly with the popularly held view of the superiority of their own race over the Africans. They therefore sought to discredit the educated Africans, who were an immediate challenge to their own position.

The fate of the majority of the Bombay Africans in the CMS mission stations hung in the balance in 1880–1881. The Consul General at Zanzibar, Sir John Kirk, had blamed them for causing friction between the missions and the Arabs on the coast by harbouring runaway slaves. The Consul did not realise that the Bombay Africans and particularly their leaders, William Jones and

79

George David, were more concerned with the freedom of a large number of their fellow Africans than with obeying the laws that kept them enslaved.

At Salisbury Square it seemed likely that the racists and opponents of African church leadership who would later cause the disgrace of Bishop Crowther, would triumph and that the purge that was to come to the Niger Mission, in 1890–1891, would be anticipated. A special commission was set up to inquire into the difficulties of the Mombasa Mission.[31] Two problems were involved First there was the charge levelled against the missionaries at Mombasa by the Consul for usurping the authority of the Sultan and also the charge of excess cruelty to the freed slaves and to the subjects of the Sultan over whom Streeter had no jurisdiction. There was also the question of the relationship between the missionaries and the Bombay Africans which had already reached breaking point and which led to the Bombay Africans' memorandum of 1881.

Two independent inquiries were set up at the same time: one by the Consul General at Zanzibar, on request from the Sultan,[32] and the other, by the CMS at Salisbury Square, who chose William Price as their special commissioner. He was instructed to inquire into the charges brought against the missionaries by the Arabs. But of more concern to the Bombay Africans, he was instructed to inquire into the administration of the mission and to recommend its future prospects. In particular, he was instructed to 'consider whether in the interest of the community, it may not be necessary to remove, as soon as possible, from the mission stations, some of the Bombay Africans who appear to have given trouble.'[33]

But Price, who had lived with the Bombay Africans both in India and Africa, was unlikely to make rash recommendations about them, nor was he likely to recommend the abandonment of Freretown and Rabai by the CMS. He was so intimately connected with both of them that he would not have wanted the work he had laboured for to be abandoned.

William Price came out from England in December, 1881 and carried out his inquiry into the mission early in 1882. The missionaries at Mombasa did not like his appointment as a special commissioner. The Rev. Menzies, for example, did not give him the customary welcome always offered to fellow missionaries from England. Price noted: 'The fact that the Reverend Menzies knew of my coming a month ago and that three messengers came from him to Zanzibar after my arrival there without a line of welcome to me was not encouraging.'[34]

In his report Price agreed with Frederick Holmwood who was appointed by the Consul-General to enquire into the charges levelled against the missionaries by the Arabs, that the lay superintendent, A. J. Streeter, was guilty. He also agreed with the recommendation that all three missionaries at Freretown should be removed in the interests of the mission.

The major portion of his report dealt with the Mombasa Mission. Regarding the future prospects of the mission, he emphatically recommended an increase of white missionaries and suggested making Freretown the headquarters of all the CMS missions in East Africa.

Victor Buxton, who visited East Africa in 1904 many years after Price's recommendation, wrote of the urgent need for more missionaries for pioneer work in the Mombasa Mission but stressed that there, as in Uganda, the task could only be effectively accomplished by means of a devoted native agency. He affirmed that it was this consideration which gave special weight to the work at Freretown where they were training school masters, catechists and pastors. Price's recommendation for the increase of resident European missionaries at Mombasa was good, and he made it in good faith.

But the increase of resident European missionaries would automatically lessen the opportunities for Bombay Africans to rise into positions of responsibility in the mission. Price stressed and reiterated Venn's policy that wherever there was a native congregation a native pastor should be ordained, to minister to it.[35] There was already a large African congregation at Freretown and Rabai and there were also George David, William Jones and Ishmael Seimler, all in charge of mission stations or sub-stations. Since they had many years of experience, Price felt that they should already have been ordained. In particular he blamed the CMS for denying George David, then in charge of Kamlikeni stations, the responsibility commensurate with the duties he was performing. Price stated emphatically:

They are spiritually minded, possess many gifts and qualifications, speak English and Swahili, and for more than fifteen years have worked faithfully, have the confidence and respect of Native Christians, and Native Congregations should be under native pastors.[36]

William Price felt that the creation of the post of lay superintendent had tended to separate the secular side of the mission from the more important spiritual aspect of it. The lay superintendent, he felt, had acted far too independently of the missionary in charge and had administered the mission like a military camp. Instead, he advised the appointment of a more senior person to be in charge of the Mombasa Mission. His recommendation was put into effect in 1884 with the creation of the Bishopric of East Equatorial Africa centred at Freretown.

Of the Bombay Africans, Price wrote, 'The facts speak for themselves. It may well be asked where should we be now but for the valuable help which these men and women have given and are giving.'[37] In his report he included a table of the posts the Bombay Africans were holding in the mission to show that they held all the positions of trust. William Price was not, therefore, the man to recommend the removal of those Bombay Africans whom, after all, he had brought up and taught in their early youth in Bombay and with whom he had worked side by side at Mombasa after 1874.

At the UMCA Cathedral in Zanzibar, where he attended a Kishwahili service en route to Mombasa, he found that

The most respectable part of (the congregation) was composed of Bombay African Christians. Most of them for one reason or another have been turned out of Freretown and found refuge and regular employment with Dr Steere. He gladly avails himself of these men and women. It does seem a pity that those whom we have trained ... should be lost to us in this way but I cannot think they have been dealt with wisely or fairly. It is very hard to force them into a position in which they have to choose between virtually giving themselves with a Mission with ritualistic practice of which they have no sympathy.[38]

William Jones, who had remained in the mission, later remarked that the missionaries at the time had depopulated the mission and forced freed slaves out to suit their own evil purposes. He sadly reported:

Of the 300 Makua who were landed at Freretown ten years ago ... 100 have been driven away between the time of Streeter and Mr Handford (schoolmaster at Rabai during the time of trouble with the Bombay Africans) and only eight of them now left and perhaps less ... those who were sent away during Mr Handford's time, it was just to suit his purposes. The God of Justice judged Mr Handford because he was arrested in Zanzibar with the native woman he was trying to run away with ...[39]

The Bombay Africans had migrated into the coastal towns of Mombasa and Zanzibar in 1881-1882; like the Sierra Leoneans in West Africa in the 1840s, they were too few to form viable Christian communities that would have any impact on the predominantly Muslim towns. Migration here was towards the towns, especially Mombasa and Zanzibar, where there were opportunities for work as artisans, domestic servants or retailers, and some of them had joined the UMCA and the Holy Ghost Fathers.

There is no record of their migration into the tribal interior at this early date in their history. With regard to the Makua freed slaves of whom William Jones speaks, we can surmise that the fate of a large number of them was the same as that of the Bombay Africans. It is possible, however, that a few migrated into the interior only to be absorbed in the tribal society.

But in one particular way the development of Freretown differed sharply from that of Sierra Leone and, therefore, put the Bombay Africans at a great disadvantage. Moreover, it presaged the failure of the Christian settlement from the very beginning. Unlike Sierra Leone, Freretown was not declared a British colony when it was made a freed slave settlement in 1874. The permanence and the success of Sierra Leone as a freed slave colony was ensured in 1807 when it passed from the Sierra Leone Company to Crown rule. In 1853 the freed slaves were legally allowed to own land and property and above all they could be sued and tried in British courts. The result of the establishment of Crown rule over Sierra Leone was that the freed slaves were to be accorded freedom and protection under the British Common Law and the Christian religion. As a Crown colony Sierra Leone was protected by the British government from external attack and internally the Crown ensured that the inhabitants were accorded freedom and given protection under the Crown government law.

The freed slave settlement at Mombasa was not placed under Crown rule from the beginning. The British government does not seem to have bothered to define the status of Freretown nor that of freed slaves. The situation on the East Coast made it even more necessary that, if the settlement were to survive, it had to come into British hands and the status of freed slaves had to be clearly defined. Here on the East African Coast, the freed slave settlement was planted in the middle of a Muslim-administered coastal population, loosely falling under the sovereignty of the Sultan of Zanzibar. The territory immediately adjacent to the coastal area was governed by tribal authority. According to the existing law on the entire coast, slavery was recognised. The British government, however, did not seem to have seen the necessity to move away from their traditional policy of support for the laws of the Sultan. They were content to pay the missions regular visits and warships, it was understood, were to pay them demonstrative visits too. But the frequency with which the promise was kept depended upon the availability of transport to Mombasa and relief from pressure of work at Zanzibar and elsewhere. European missionaries were accorded the same British protection as any other British citizen. But the British Consul at Zanzibar clearly told the missionaries at Mombasa, as late as 1889, that the freed slaves were not British citizens and they were therefore not entitled to British protection, so that the only recourse that any of them had against the Sultan or those in the interior was in the Arab or native courts.[40] By 1882 it was clear that George David was not to be the future Crowther of East Africa. In 1884 when the Bishopric of East Equatorial Africa was created, with its headquarters at Freretown James Hannington was consecrated its first bishop. By this time imperialism and the ideas of social Darwinism were at their peak, and the European 'scramble' for East Africa had begun. The appointment of a British bishop ended any hopes that there would ever be a black bishop in East Africa for many years to come. From then on it became clear that the Bombay Africans who had remained on the stations in 1881 and any of the freed slaves who were training as teachers and evangelists were to be relegated to inferior positions in the church. The policy of the CMS to emulate the Sierra Leone experiment, therefore, was cut short by imperialism and by the occupation of East Africa by European powers in the late 1880s.

Fortunately for the CMS, William Jones, Ishmael Seimler and George David did not leave the stations in 1880–1882. They were holding posts of responsibility at Freretown and Rabai and it would certainly have been to their disadvantage to start life afresh in Zanzibar or elsewhere. The CMS, for its part, moved ahead and approved that the two catechists, William Jones and Ishmael Seimler, should be ordained deacons (George David had died in 1884). Both Seimler and Jones were ordained deacons on Trinity Sunday, June 1885. James Hannington had come out the same year and this was his first ordination.

'I can hardly tell you,' wrote the bishop, 'how greatly privileged I feel in thus having been permitted to ordain the first native ministers of our infant East African Church. The foundations of a native ministry have now been laid.[41] In 1896 Bishop Tucker admitted to deacon orders James Deimler, the first of the Freretown freed slaves. At Rabai and Freretown, the number of Bombay Africans was by this time reduced to a minimum and their role still continued, as already seen, to be that of individuals. The addition of one of the freed slaves at Freretown into the hierarchy of deacons added the voice of the freed slaves to what had hitherto been that of the Bombay Africans only.

In the nineties mission employees of the two groups, the Bombay Africans who were left (there are no records of their number) and the freed slaves in general, coalesced into a single group and formed a Welfare Association known as the African Workers' Council, under James Deimler.[42] The first reference to the African Council appears in the CMS minutes of 1901. It seems very likely that it was formed in the nineties when the catechists, teachers, readers, and lay agents working for the mission felt a need to come together to press for their rights and to look after their own interests as a group. The CMS at Mombasa seem to have begun to discourage the teaching of English to the young African agents, much against the wishes of all the African teachers and catechists. There was also the introduction of the native dress (kanzu) that Binns wrote about and Bishop Tucker pressed for and which the African workers of the CMS resisted. There is enough reason, therefore, to believe that the African Workers' Council dates back much earlier than its first reference in the minutes of the Finance Committee of the Executive Council at Mombasa. In 1901 the Rev. Burt, secretary of the CMS, Mombasa Mission, thought it began in the early nineties when the Africans felt the mission was interfering with their lawful rights by dictating what kind of clothes they might wear and other similar matters. European paternalism, which the Bombay Africans were objecting to, was already at its peak and was to become a permanent feature in the relationship between the Africans and Europeans for the next five decades of the 20th century.

The African Workers' Council was essentially a welfare association, interested primarily in maintaining and promoting the interests of those working for the CMS Mombasa Mission as Christian agents in all sorts of capacities. The Workers' Council naturally drew its members from the freed slaves, both young and old. They were the only agents for the mission, and when the mission expanded into the highlands the first agents came from among the first Christians from the coast. As a welfare association, therefore, its interest would be to help the younger members to get used to the job and to help them stay on and, perhaps above all, to press for better conditions of service in the mission.

The Workers' Council was faced with the urgent problem of securing higher wages for the agents in the late 1890s. These agents were already complaining that the wages the mission paid were miserably low. By 1899 all peaceful pressure and negotiations for the mission to increase their wages seemed to have failed and most of the agents resigned. Bishop Peel found, on his arrival at Mombasa as the first holder of the newly-created Bishop of Mombasa, that the two Africans in Priestly Orders, William Jones and Ishmael Seimler, and the lay agents had already resigned and that James Deimler and the remaining leading licensed lay readers had also sent in their resignations.[43] Alarmed, the Executive Council of the CMS quickly moved to increase their wages. All African priests were to receive sixty rupees per month, deacons fifty rupees, village pastors between forty and fifty rupees, senior catechists thirty, Junior catechists twenty-five and evangelists between eighteen and twenty rupees.[44]

It was the solidarity of the African workers of the CMS as a group which helped them to secure recognition. Certainly it made the Executive Committee aware of the importance and power of the Workers' Council. This solidarity proved strong enough to constitute a threat to the authority of the CMS towards the turn of the century. The African Workers' Council had certainly fostered the spirit of independence which Bishop Peel witnessed among the leading African Christians in 1899. It appeared to be so strong that he felt the Africans were soon going to assert their independence. Peel cautioned the CMS to refrain from unduly asserting its authority over them as it would provoke them into action.

During the first year of the new century the authority of the Executive Committee of the CMS seemed threatened by the Workers' Council so much that it commissioned its secretary, the Rev. Burt, to enquire from the Rev. James Deimler the purpose of the Workers' Council, its rules and members. In the previous meeting of the Executive Committee held in March, one of its more over-anxious members, J. E. Hamshere, who seemed to have had trouble with the members of the African Workers' Council, believed the council was a great threat to the authority of the mission. He moved that

> the Executive Committee having had brought before them a case where certain agents had allegedly, while delaying to comply with the Committee's direction in a matter that they had referred to the African Workers' Council, the Committee desire, affectionately to point out to all the Society's Agents under them that no Association should be allowed by the Agents to come in as a third party between them individually and the Society under whom they serve. . . .[45]

The other members of the Executive Committee did not feel that there was sufficient evidence for them to support the resolution although they passed it on to Salisbury Square at the request of Hamshere. The committee, however, asked the Secretary, F. Burt, to find out from James Deimler about the council. Deimler's response to these questions did not seem to satisfy the Executive Committee. In the committee meeting of July 4, 1901 Burt reported that 'he had written back to Mr Deimler to write clearer answers to the questions asked by the Executive Committee.'[46]

In his first response to the committee's questions, James Deimler had said that the purpose of the council was to help its members to consider and to report to the bishop of the Executive Committee what they thought was the best method of carrying on their work, and to encourage young beginners to persevere in their work. The council forbade individual members to answer a difficult matter and no one was to resign before consultation with the council whose decision was binding. Finally, the council was open to pastors, catechists and readers.[47] These were the moderate and unambitious objects of the welfare association. But the Executive Committee, already suspicious that the Council had political aims, requested James Deimler to give fuller answers. However Deimler failed to respond.

Several interpretations are possible to explain the anxiety of the Executive Committee of the CMS at Mombasa about the African Workers' Council. One was evidently their desire to contain and channel any African movement in the direction they themselves wanted it to take and one which would work in their favour. Bishop Peel advocated this line of approach in 1900 for he said that 'this spirit of independence ... in leading African Christians, if rightly and lovingly guided, will be of estimable importance in the near future.'[48] CMS missionaries were, therefore, to patronise and fraternise with any African movements or associations. Archdeacon Owen, years later, came to patronise the Kavirondo Welfare Association in a manner which diverted its political goals and notably distinguished it from the politically militant Young Kikuyu Central Association which was not patronised by European missionaries. The missionaries, therefore, wanted to redirect African political movements into purely welfare associations that would not challenge their own authority.

Another possible explanation might well be that they expected civil disobedience. They wanted, therefore, to forestall it by expelling the more militant leaders. The CMS was less likely to adopt repression, for the bishop had previously warned them against it. Moreover, it could not do so without crippling its work since it would be faced with mass resignations and desertions by African agents. Fear of repression was most probably the reason why Deimler avoided giving the list of the members of the council.

The African Workers' Council proved to be the last activity of any significant nature organised by the Bombay Africans and the

Reverend W. S. Price

Boys' School Freretown

بمنه تعالي

Deed of Freedom of *Machoo mi Mana Miginda*

No. 361

الي كافة من يراه وبعد فان هذه نجومي مانا الجنديه

، كانت مملوكه والأن صارت حرة ما لاحد عليها تعرض

حرر في ٢١ من شهر   ١٢٩٢

Dated at 21st *Rajab* 1292

The 25 *August* 187

H. M'S. AGENT & CONSUL GENERAL.

Slave's Deed of Freedom

freed slaves in general. The end of the freed slaves as an important group in the CMS mission stations had already come that year (1901) when the CMS began work in the highlands. The death of William Jones in 1904 ended the era of mission work among the freed slaves. It also ended the era of Bombay Africans, that small but vocal and important group of liberated slaves on the Mombasa Coast. They had not produced the grand results produced by their counterparts on the West Coast. However, they had made a significant contribution to the work of the CMS in Kenya. The freed slaves themselves almost completely disappeared after 1907 when slavery was abolished in the East African Protectorate.

NOTES

1. Eugene Stock, *History of the Church Missionary Society*, 4 vols. (London, 1899–1916), Vol. II, p. 431.
2. W. Price to Hutchison, July 19, 1873, C A5/017, CMS Archives, London.
3. CMS Proceedings, 1867/68, pp. 49–50.
4. CMS Proceedings, 1865/67, p. 82
5. Bartle Frere to Granville, April 5, 1873, FO 84/1390, PRO.
6. Price to Lang, August 29, 1888, G3 A5/05 CMS Archives, London.
7. Lamb to Wright, June 16, 1876, C A5/67.
8. Handford to Lang, October 1, 1884, CMS Archives, London.
9. W. Jones to Secretary, October 10, 1878, C A5/014 CMS Archives, London.
10. George David to Wright, 'Report on a Visit to Godoma,' September 27, 1875, C A5/06 CMS Archives, London.
11. *Ibid.*
12. Jones to Wright, August 7, 1878, C A5/014, CMS Archives, London.
13. *Ibid.*
14. Price to Lang, May 25, 1885, G3 A5/05, CMS Archives, London.
15. Morris to Price, March 7, 1888, G3 A5/05, CMS Archives, London.
16. Kilifi Political Records, Vol. I, 1913 Kenya National Archives, Nairobi.
17. Jones to Wright, October 10, 1878, C A5/014 CMS Archives, London.
18. Jones to Bishop Peel, November 27, 1902, in file marked 'Letters to 1913,' Archbishop of East Africa's Archives, CMS Nairobi (Cited hereafter as Bishop's Archives, CMS Nairobi).
19. John Iliffe, 'The Age of Improvement and Differentiation' in Kimambo and Temu, ed. *History of Tanzania* p. 141.
20. Jones to Wright *op. cit.*
21. *Ibid.*
22. E. C. Dawson, *James Hannington, First Bishop of East Equatorial Africa: A History of his Life and Work, 1847–1885* (London, 1887), p. 396.

D

23. *Ibid.*, p. 396.
24. Lamb to Wright, November 4, 1876, C A5/017, CMS Archives, London.
25. Lamb to Wright, October 9, 1876, C A5/017, CMS Archives, London.
26. Streeter to Hutchinson, November 18, 1880, C A5/027, CMS Archives, London.
27. Menzies to Wright, February 4, 1881, G3 A5/01, CMS Archives, London.
28. Bombay Africans' Memorandum to the Secretary, CMS Salisbury Square, May 19, 1881, G3 A5/01, CMS Archives, London. (Cited hereafter as Bombay Africans' Memorandum).
29. Menzies to Stock, May 20, 1881, G3 A5/01, CMS Archives, London.
30. W. G. Peel to CMS, 'Report on the Mombasa Mission,' (not dated), 1900, G3 A5/106, CMS Archives, London.
31. Bombay Africans' Memorandum.
32. Lang to Price, 'Instructions to W. S. Price Proceeding to Freretown as Special Commissioner of CMS,' November 11, 1881, C A5/L2, CMS Archives, London.
33. John Kirk to Granville, July 1, 1881, FO 541/49, PRO.
34. Lang to Price, November 11, 1881, C A5/L2, CMS Archives, London.
35. Price to Wingram, January 4, 1882, G3 A5/01, CMS Archives.
36. Price Report 1882 pp. 2–3.
37. *Ibid.*
38. *Ibid.*, pp. 5–6.
39. *Ibid.*
40. Jones to Wingram, October 15, 1886, G3 A5/04, CMS Archives, London.
41. Price to Wingram, December 14, 1881, G3 A5/01, CMS Archives, London.
42. Downes Shaw to Lang, October 15, 1889, G3 A5/06, CMS Archives, London.
43. Dawson, p. 363.
44. Minutes of the Executive Committee, Mombasa Mission, July 12, 1901, in file marked 'Diocese of Mombasa—Cumulative Minutes,' Bishop's Archives, CMS Nairobi.
45. W. G. Peel to CMS, 'Report on the Mombasa Mission,' (not dated), 1900, G3 G5/016, CMS Archives, London.
46. Harry Binns to Baylis, January 19, 1900, G3 A5/015, CMS Archives, London.
47. Minutes of the Executive Committee, Mombasa Mission, July 12, 1901 in file marked 'Diocese of Mombasa—Cumulative Minutes,' Bishop's Archives, CMS, Nairobi.
48. *Ibid.*, July 4, 1901.
49. J. Deimler to Burt, June 14, 1901, Enclosure in Minutes of Executive Committee, Mombasa Mission, July 4, 1901, Bishop's Archives, Nairobi.
50. W. G. Peel to CMS 'Report on the Mombasa Mission,' (not dated), 1900, G3 A5/016, CMS Archives, London.

5

Missionary Expansion, the Acquisition of Land and the Disruption of African Society, 1900-1914

At the beginning of the century the forms of activity not only in administration but also in the missions moved from Mombasa to the highlands. The completion of the East African railway in 1901 caused a pell-mell race among the missions into hitherto un-occupied territory.[1] The fact that the missionaries, journeying to Uganda, did not see fit to start evangelical work in the com-mercial centres established by the company serves only to emphasise that the missions, like the officials of the British East Africa Company aimed only at reaching Buganda. William Price had urged the CMS as early as 1888 to keep their eyes open and to make the best use of the road the company was surveying. In 1889 Price established a mission station at Gulu, where the com-pany had established a post.[2] However, the CMS and the UMFC did not live up to this. Protestant mission expansion to the highlands, therefore, followed the railway and the British administration.

Between 1900 and 1910 mission stations were established across the highlands. The extensive territory, hitherto known as the diocese of East Equatorial Africa, was divided into two in 1899. Alfred Tucker retained the bishopric of Uganda, and George Peel became the new bishop of Mombasa diocese. Nyanza Province remained in the bishopric of Uganda, and the CMS areas in Tanganyika in that of Mombasa. In the following year Bishop Peel visited the Kikuyu, and A. W. MacGregor transferred from Taveta to Fort Smith on October 13, 1900, moving to found a permanent station at Kihuruko the following year.[3] Following closely, CMS stations were founded at Weithaga in 1903, Kahuhia in 1906, Mahiga in 1908 and Embu in 1910.[4] Effective work among the Luo in Nyanza Province began in 1906, when Archdeacon J. J. Willis, who later became the second bishop of Uganda (after Alfred Tucker), was posted there.[5]

The United Methodists moved to the highlands in 1910 and established their first station at Meru that year. Another newcomer, but preceding the CMS by one year, was the Church of Scotland Mission (CSM). The CSM moved from Kibwezi in 1898 and established themselves at Nairobi, west of the escarpment, that year.[6] By the end of the decade all three major British Protestant missions had established themselves on the highlands, indeed had made the highlands the centre of their missions. Other missions, such as the Holy Ghost Mission and the Consolata Mission, also came. The missionaries of the Holy Ghost established a mission station in Kiambu where they began to grow coffee. The Institute of Consolata sent out its first missionaries to Kenya in 1902 and started work in Kiambu, Fort Hall and Nyeri. The missionaries embarked on the establishment of a coffee plantation in Nyeri where they acquired 3 000 acres of land.[7] From America came the missionaries of the African Inland Mission and those of the Gospel Missionary Society.[8]

On the coast this should have been a period of bustling activity, for the pioneer period was long past. But most missionaries confessed, during the turn of the century, that their work there had been a failure. The United Methodists, years later, admitted that the coastal regions 'chiefly because of malaria, cannot maintain a large population and that our missions there cannot be expected to grow much beyond its present population.'[9] In future, they recommended the centre of work should be in the highlands.

The two oldest Protestant Missions had produced some results of consequence before the shift became complete. For one thing, the few missionaries among the Wanyika and Wataita, or on the Tana River working among the Wapokomo, had, by the 1890s, become well-known throughout the area and the nearest tribes had begun to take them into their confidence. There, they often acted as administrators and collectors of tax, serving as agents of the colonial administration. Sir Charles Eliot, the Commissioner for the East Africa Protectorate, was able to report in 1902 that the administration had gained greatly from the missions. He particularly praised the efforts they had expended in spreading civilisation among the African peoples, and especially the assistance they had rendered in exhorting their congregations to pay the recently introduced hut tax.[10]

Mr Moss Omeroid and Mr John Consterdine served as interpreters and advisers to the administration and often helped to popularise government regulations and objectives to the Pokomo. Particularly significant was the fact that in 1897 Mr Andersen, Sub-Commissioner, had promulgated three orders whose acceptance and understanding by the Pokomo depended on the advice and approval of the missionaries there.[11] One order required that all traders on the Tana River be licensed, those concerned being required to deposit some money as a guarantee of good conduct. The second order directed that natives with food to dispose of had to sell it to the government to ensure that there was surplus food in case of famine; and the third order prohibited advances in cash made on growing crops or the supply of goods on credit to soldiers.[12] The three decrees were not controversial. In essence thay aimed at protecting the Pokomo and the advice the missionaries gave them—to accept the decrees—did not provoke the suspicion which a controversial decree, touching their interests, would have done.

Partly because of shortage of civil personnel, and partly because the missionary and the administrator did much the same thing in the initial period, it was not necessary for there to be a civil administrator in every district. The government, therefore, relied heavily on the missions.[13] Eliot acknowledged this comity of interest between the government and the missions. He said:

the opening of a new mission station has seemed to me to be generally as efficacious for the extension of European influence as the opening of a Government station and there are districts in East Africa, such as Teita and the lower Tana, in which European influence has hitherto been represented almost entirely by the missionaries, but which have made as great progress as the regions which have been taken in hand by Government officials.[14]

Sixteen years later District Commissioner Tate recommended that the CSM take over the administration of Chuka on the Meru-Kikuyu boundary for similar reasons.[15]

The two Protestant missions had stressed the agricultural side of their occupation as a means of training their converts and of supporting the missions. This was in line with what David Livingstone had advocated, namely, Christianity through capitalism, trade and white settlement. To this end the British Protestant missions acquired large areas of land on which they raised commercial crops. On the coast the amount of land acquired varied from place to place. The United Methodists there had embarked on commercial agriculture on an appreciable scale. They had 6 000 acres of land in the River Tana region, 750 at Ribe and another 500 acres at Mazera.[16] They grew rubber and coconuts on the three estates and also, at Mazeras, they grew fruit for sale at Mombasa. By the turn of the century the Methodists had achieved a notable success in commercial farming, and in 1910 the District Commissioner of Malindi, R. Skene, reported that the estate of the Methodists at Ribe was the best in the district. The mission had planted 22,000 rubber trees out of which it hoped to realise £1 000 during the year.

Next to the Methodists in commercial undertakings came the CSM; although it was a late-comer to the coast its work was short-lived. In 1891 the East Africa Scottish Mission was established at Kibwezi, about 200 miles from Mombasa, on the initiative of the British East Africa Company.[17] The directors of the company wanted the mission to be religious, educational, medical and industrial. Dr James Stewart of Lovedale was transferred from Nyasaland to found Kibwezi and to be the first superintendent of the East Africa Scottish Mission. Land was acquired from Chief Kilundu of the Wakamba, and the British East Africa Company set aside 100 square miles to the mission on which to develop agriculture and industries.[18] The mission was supposed to make a physical contribution to the company by training Africans in industrial arts. Almost at once the mission began to train the Africans in brick-making, carpentry and masonry, and also began experimenting with a coffee plantation on its huge estate. Very little evangelical work was achieved there and the mission became essentially a supply depot of porters for caravans en-route to Uganda.[19]

The Kibwezi Mission was an industrial mission of the IBEAC

94

and though imbued with humanitarianism, characteristic of William Mackinnon and the rest of the directors of the company, it was a commercial undertaking *per se.* Due to harsh climatic conditions and to the scanty Akamba population, which was not apparent in 1891, Thomas Watson was commissioned to negotiate for the disposal of Kibwezi.[20] He was instructed to acquire a new site in Kikuyu, near the railway and the administration, high up on the escarpment west of Nairobi. In 1900 the mission already acquired was placed under the direction of the Church of Scotland Foreign Mission Committee. Thomas Watson had reported in 1899 that he aimed to begin with as much land as possible, '600 acres, if the government charges only nominal rent since it is the best way of getting hold of the natives.'[21] Before the end of the decade Henry Scott from Blantyre, now superintendent of the Kikuyu Mission, had acquired 3 000 acres of land and had opened a second station at Tumutumu in 1908.[22]

The CMS did not embark on agricultural and industrial undertakings before the beginning of the twentieth century. During the second half of the 1890s the idea of developing industries in East Africa and Uganda on a commercial basis was mooted by the CMS. When Bishop Peel arrived in the protectorate to take over the diocese of Mombasa, he felt there was a great need for industrial enterprise. Industries, he believed, would give his adherents work to do and also help the economy of the new colony. He wrote:

> On my arrival in British East Africa at the close of 1899, a great field for industrial enterprise presented itself. The Freretown settlement of the CMS ... had many Christians who had nothing to look for beyond a little patch of ground in which to raise some beans and maize. In Rabai ... there were numerous Christians similarly situated. These limitations engendered idleness, contributed to poverty and failed to draw the man into activities which are the health of a community.[23]

Besides, the railway called for production, and the needy colonial administration continuously called for the country to contribute to the treasury. The bishop felt that this call was directed to the mission as well as to the new settlers.

The bishop appealed to the Industrial Aid Mission Society (IAMS), in England, to begin industries in East Africa. The East African Industries Limited finally emerged in 1906 and established industries at Freretown, Dabinda and Maseno. At Mombasa the IAMS had 2 000 acres of land and at Maseno a 1 000 acre farm.[24] E. J. Harrison came out at the turn of the century as superintendent of the new company at Mombasa. Brick-making, castor oil, coconut and copra industries were got under way on the estate.[25] Commissioner Eliot and his commercial adviser, Marsden, had recommended establishing small industries to stave off the bishop's fear that they would be forced out by large capitalist-backed schemes. Peel hailed the initiation of the company as

a great encouragement to all who have industrial missions at heart, it being easy to discern the promise of material prosperity of converts and children of converts, while at the same time it is inspiring to know that these facilities of labour will be in connection with God-fearing white men who will seek to engage the workman's whole man in the glorifying of God. The industries now open in the Protectorate are many. Government is offering lots of 640 acres free in certain locations to those who will undertake the growing of cotton, vanilla, rubber, coffee, etc.[26]

Protestant missions to Kenya adopted agriculture and industry for their economic self-sufficiency and as one means of evangelising the Africans. The missions, it has already been stated, had been allowed to settle and build on tribal land. It is true that they paid for the land in the form of cloth, wire, beads, etc. To the African chiefs or elders such permission did not mean permanent cession of their land to the foreigner but only a temporary residence amidst the tribe from which they certainly hoped to gain politically and economically. Gradually, and more seriously, but without the sanction of the tribe, the missions extended their area to include more land which later amounted to thousands of acres. Typical of this mission zest for land were the CSM. 'We must not just be content with small means,' wrote W. S. Mclachlan, secretary of the Foreign Missions Central Committee, 'but perhaps you may be able to get ... more land.'[27] The United Methodist Church could claim in 1910 that they had purchased about 6 000 acres of freehold land at Golbanti from the Galla in 1884.[28]

The missionaries used the Crown Lands Ordinance that was issued in Kenya in 1902 to secure a permanent claim to the land they had been given freely by the Africans. The Ordinance allowed for the alienation of land in Kenya for white settlement and laid down very liberal conditions under which land could be secured. The Act vested power for the alienation of land in the Commissioner for the Protectorate. A particular cause for alarm was that the Act provided for the Commissioner to grant leases of land containing native villages or settlements without specifically excluding the settlements.

The missionaries easily obtained certificates of occupation from the Commissioner. Further, all the missions joined in the race to extend the land they already had, to acquire more new estates in the highlands. Whether small or large estates, they put forward the claim that they were for mission purposes. The provision in the 1902 Act, that areas of land containing native villages or settlements could be alienated without excluding them, was particularly suited to the purposes of the missionaries. It gave them control of the Africans whom they could easily force to become Christians as a condition for settling on what had become mission land. There was also a labour force to develop the estate, labour which the missionaries made a condition for remaining on the land. So the Africans, who ceased to be owners of this land, reverted to being tenants under the new masters. They were faced with eviction unless they fulfilled the conditions required of them as tenants.

In 1908 Dr Henry Scott, superintendent of the Church of Scotland Kikuyu mission, entered into an agreement with 81 tenants, original owners of the mission estate, in the presence of the District Commissioner at Dagoretti. The tenants agreed to work for the mission for two months every year in return for subsistence on the estate. Dr Scott further agreed to pay them four rupees per month.[29] In the following year he introduced the indentured system of labour on the estate. But when he further required his tenants to send their children to school, many of them chose to leave the mission estate rather than succumb to this demand.[30]

All the missions adopted similar procedures with variations to

D*

suit their particular needs. But the United Methodist Society boasted in 1912 that it was not dependent on indentured labour for its estates, and expressed strong disapproval of every form of indentured labour.[31] However, it urged missionaries to reach the labourers on the estates. But in the early 1920s when they felt the pinch of the shortage of labour under extensive developments, they forced their tenants to work for them. At Jilore, where the CMS had 1 000 acres of land, the mission demanded that those cultivating the mission land had to pay a rental of between one and five shillings per year. And to induce pagans to become Christians the CMS made special rates for the Christians on their land.[32]

Until 1904 the Foreign office and the protectorate government had not begun the policy of establishing native reserves. That year Sir Donald Stewart, who succeeded Sir Charles Eliot as governor, was instructed by the Foreign Office to set up reserves for the Masai.[33] Later two reserves, one south of Ngong and the railway, railway was thrown open for European settlement. In 1909 the other north, on the Laikipia plains, were set aside for the Masai, while the intervening territory on Lake Naivasha along the Girouard recommended a system of defined, inalienable reserves, and some districts had already been set aside for the Nandi, Kikuyu and the tribes on the coast. The Land Titles Act of 1908 was enacted to cement it. Under this Act an attempt was made to adjudicate and record titles before allowing alienation.

Over on the highlands pressure from settlers was mounting for the alienation of land demarcated as Masai reserve on the Laikipia plains. The government on the spot, with the backing of the missions, seemed in favour of establishing one reserve for the Masai. The missions in the highlands believed that the concentration of the Masai and, for that matter, of any tribe, into one reserve would facilitate their work among the tribe as it would give them large concentrations of people whom they could easily reach. Hitherto the missions had been unsuccessful among the Masai because they were widely scattered over a very extensive area.

The policy of native reserves and, in consequence, the large and important one of demarcating special and distinct areas for the different races, began with the Masai. But once begun, a precedent was established for the restriction of the other tribes. However. it

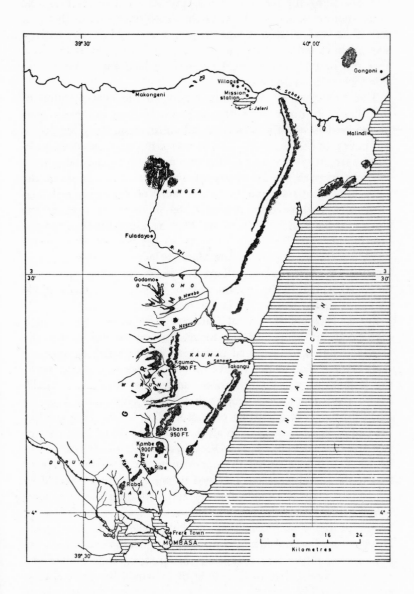

Location Sketch: African catechists in areas and villages around the Kenya coast

was one thing for the governor to proclaim native reserves, and quite another to respect them, for he could offer land in them for sale if he was satisfied it was no longer required by the natives. The missions did not keep out of the reserves. Indeed, if they had kept out of them they would not have gained any converts outside their mission estates.

The Protestant missions fully supported the concentration of the Masai into one reserve, thus giving a blessing to the demands of the settlers and the pro-settler administration. They supported the policy from what they argued was a moral point of view. In April 1910, at the meeting held between the Masai and the government to prepare for the treaty of 1911, Dr Henry Scott of the Church of Scotland, and C. E. Hurlburt of the African Inland Mission, were invited to represent the missions. Writing to the Governor, Sir Percy Girouard on May 1, immediately after the meeting in which they were a party to the pressure the government brought to bear upon the Masai to agree to move into one reserve, Dr Scott said, 'Hurlburt ... holds the same view as I do ... [that] it is in the best interests of the Masai tribe as a whole that they should be together in one reserve. . . .'[34]

Bishop Peel put the moral Christian view even more sharply. Like Scott, he supported the move, but on condition that the area was suited to them and that there was enough pasturage for their cattle.[35] To put the Masai into one reserve was, according to the bishop, 'sound administration and a wise step in the moulding of these remarkable peoples afresh in a civilisation, Western and Christian, but admitting of conservation of anything good in the end of keeping them from all the peculiar evils of their present system and customs.'[36] The Vicar Apostolic of Zanzibar and British East Africa seized the opportunity to warn the governor that if the Masai were not confined to one reserve they would be a major source of trouble for the administration in the future. Echoing the Protestant missions' view, he wrote, 'you are only aware of the moral condition of the people if they are once brought together and firmly controlled by government.[37] Thus far it had been difficult to evangelise this pastoral tribe and so the missions believed that work among them would be easier if they were restricted in one area.

It is unfortunate that the heads of the missions in Kenya should have so unanimously supported the initiation and execution of a policy of segregation and establishment of separate areas for the different races. Had they had the foresight to look beyond the narrow limits of evangelisation and into the future of Kenya in so far as the relationship of the two races and their welfare was concerned, they surely would have advocated a wiser policy. No doubt their thinking followed the same line as that of their counterparts in Northern Rhodesia and Southern Africa.

By 1914 all of the missions had applied for and taken up land on the reserves on which to build a church; and some, like the Church of Scotland and the Consolata Mission, had taken up huge areas of land for commercial purposes. The Kikuyu whose reserves were being invaded were concerned because the missions were taking the most fertile and cultivated land, often near the rivers. Bishop Peel said the administration was stirred by the way in which some missionaries were going into a district, getting land and building where the chief and his people did not desire it. But he exonerated the CMS from having taken part in the rape: 'CMS had not been guilty for forcing sites so far as I know and I trust never will be.'[38]

As early as 1906 the protectorate administration moved to stop encroachment on native reserves. For example, that year they refused to allow the extension of the boundary of the Church of Scotland estates as far south as Kibwezi River to include the area demarcated as Akamba reserve.[39] Writing to Scott in 1909, Hobley instructed that in the event of the Church of Scotland selling their estate, they must reserve enough land for Chief Ndege and Kitabi and their 500 people, who were already living on the estates. Over on the Tana River region where the United Free Methodists held a 6 000 acre estate, the same situation arose. There were a number of Pokomo settling on the estates with villages and shambas. The governor, however, instructed the Methodists to reserve enough land for them.[40]

In 1909 Sir Frederick Jackson, the Governor of the Protectorate, sought a ruling from the Colonial Office to define the nature and the kind of missions which should be granted land. The particular case in point was the application for land by the Mennonites, which led him to ask the Colonial Office for 'advice as to grant of land to so-called missions which [were] practically private enterprises.'[41] Lord Crewe, Under-Secretary at the Colonial Office, advised that 'missions should be treated like ordinary bodies or individuals, in connection with application for grants of land, both as to the areas to be taken up and the terms on which the land is to be held and as to districts in which such grants may be made.'[42] The Colonial Office, whose approval was necessary for a land grant in the protectorate, was certainly very generous in meeting applications for land by missionary societies. Such grants of land had been generously offered in England and the older colonies and there was, therefore, a tradition from which they could not depart, even in the twentieth century.

By the end of the decade the Kenya government was alarmed by the multiplicity of missions applying for grants of land in the country, especially in the highlands. The government was also alarmed by the chaos and confusion caused by catechists operating among the Africans, often against the will of the chief and elders.[43] Girouard submitted a list of missionary societies working in Kenya to the Colonial Office, and requested that no application from any other missionary society should be accepted without prior reference to him. He intimated that before approving any application for a missionary society to work in Kenya the society concerned should submit its financial position and its object in establishing missions in Kenya.[44]

In the highlands of Kenya the struggle to gain converts between different missions and societies established within so short a distance from one another seemed explosive. Such competition was not in the best interests of the natives they were trying to convert. In the early days of their work on the coast the Protestant missions had divided the area among themselves and each agreed to keep within its own area. When they moved to the highlands they did the same. The increase of societies and missions, however, limited their area of expansion, and they found it difficult to keep to their agreement. Moreover, the African catechists least knew what these agreements were about. The entrance of the Roman Catholics into the area further complicated the situation since they were not a party to the agreement between the British Protestant missions. The Roman Catholics argued, with justification, that if it was considered safe for a Protestant mission to establish itself in any one district or reserve, they had an equal right to open their own station in the same area.

The Kenya government intervened to prevent unnecessary competition and a possible clash between the different missions and societies. As early as 1904 the government had imposed a three-mile limit between any two different missions.[45] By 1910 the competition was so explosive that the administration imposed a ten-mile distance between any two different missions or societies. The government further ruled that no catechist could work in any area without the consent of the elders of the area or of the local authority.[46]

The Africans were surprised by the multiplicity of different sects. For one thing, they could not understand the cause for the antagonism and rancour between the different sects and societies. In African eyes they were all spreading the gospel and the difference in doctrine between the missions seemed meaningless and mystifying. Certainly the intense competition for converts and for areas of operation between them only served to confuse the Africans even more. It is no wonder then that the administration moved to curb this competition.

More importantly, the Protestant missionary societies tried to unite together in an attempt to offer to the African Christians a more uniform form of worship, prayer and baptism, in a United Church. During the first decade of the new century the Protestant missions began to be concerned about the effects on their converts of so many different sects within so close a distance of one another in the highlands. European settlements in the highlands inevitably necessitated movement of African farm-workers from the reserves to the farms and from farm to farm. The growth of Mombasa and Nairobi, with job opportunities for Africans, led to large migration from the reserves to the new towns. These migrant African workers included among them a majority of Christians belonging to different denominations. All of them were little concerned about doctrinal differences between the different missions nor did such differences make any sense to them. Most African Christians therefore attended services and received communion in the nearest church. Those who had been excommunicated from one mission joined another without any difficulty, and catechists and teachers resigned from one mission and easily found employment in another.

In 1908 the Protestant missions held their first conference at Kijabe, the African Inland Mission Station. Those represented agreed upon a common educational system and code and common translation work.[47] The following year the missions held another conference to consider the same problem. At both meetings J. J.

Willis, the Bishop of Uganda, who had consulted with Dr Henry Scott of the CSM, presented his proposals for a United African Church.[48] In 1913 the Kikuyu Conference was held at CSM Kikuyu station, at which proposals for the federation of the Protestant missions in Kenya were discussed and referred to their Home Committees for approval. Willis wrote:

The historic Conference at Kikuyu in 1913 set before the Church in East Africa a great ideal and a very difficult problem. The ideal was a single African Church, allowing for considerable varieties of organisation and worship, but united in fundamental faith, a united Church which would from the first be free from the trammels of denominational differences.[49]

The United Church was not realised, for at the conference the Bishop of Zanzibar, Frank Weston, raised issues covering the common service of Communion in which the Bishops of Mombasa and Uganda had participated. The controversy which the Anglican Bishop raised was centred on the question of the Ministry and Inter-Communion. There was much publicity about the question both in East Africa and Great Britain. The narrowness of the Anglican Bishop, Weston, and of his home authority, who could not see that such differences did not matter to those who would ultimately have to control their own church, overruled the principle of federation. It is interesting to observe that those who were concerned, that is, the African Christians of Kenya, never participated in the discussions. The controversy was silenced by the First World War.

After the war the Protestant missions met again, at Kikuyu, in 1918. Doctrinal differences between the Protestant missions seemed to have hardened, though their united efforts in the war, as seen in the Mission Volunteer Corps, ought to have taught them a lesson. As before, the African Christians who had been even more united in the war, were not brought into the conference even as observers. Here again it was the historic differences within European Protestantism that prevented the formation of a United African Church in Kenya. 'It became clear,' wrote Willis, 'that Federation was impracticable, and we fell back on an Alliance as being less rigid than a formal Federation.'[50] Four missionary societies formed the alliance: the Church of Scotland Mission, the Methodist Mission, The Church Missionary Society and the African Inland Mission, an interdenominational mission. The alliance appointed an Executive Committee known as the Representative Council.

The 1920s opened before the different Protestant missions had resolved the question of their differences. These were in themselves unimportant to the African Christians, who not only entered the 1920s with these differences but, when they took over from the white missionaries in the 1950s, inherited the European doctrinal differences as well. The alliance, it should be noted, became an influential voice of the four Protestant missions in the politics and the affairs of the country from then on.

On the eve of the First World War the numbers of Christians gained by the British Protestant missions on the highlands, not mentioning the others, could not justify their existence there. At Mombasa their presence, during most of the latter half of the nineteenth century could be accounted for by the existence of freed slaves. But by the 1890s slave-trading had been abolished; the sale and purchase of slaves and all forms of slave-trading were absolutely prohibited and no one born after January 1, 1890 could be a slave. So far there had been very little progress amongst the Nyika, not to mention the Arab population at Mombasa. For example, reference has been made to 700–800 adherents reported at Rabai, but with a minority of Warabai among them. The majority of them were ex-slaves, or their descendants. Binns, who had worked on the coast for more than thirty years, summed it up thus:

I don't mean to say that there are not true Christians, thank God, there are many, certainly several whom we know to be followers of the Lord Jesus, but these are hardly, I should think 1% of those who have been taught. Of the freed slaves' descendants, there are very few indeed of those who were brought over from India or descendants, fewer still. Of the descendants of the original Giriama country, there are few teaching in our schools or working as agents in other ways.[51]

By 1910 the CMS stations at Mombasa reported over 1 400 baptised Christians. But it is not far wrong to surmise that the baptism, as was the case at Rabai, had been attained through the excess zeal of the missionaries.

Translational work and the study of tribal tongues apart, the CMS admitted that the most outstanding feature of their work at Mombasa was its cathedral, which was dedicated in 1905, and had been built as a memorial to the first two bishops of East Equatorial Africa, James Hannington and Henry Parker, and the Secretary of CMS, Henry Wright. Eugene Stock said it was an imposing structure, with a strikingly Oriental effect.[52] There were similar cathedrals in Uganda, Zanzibar and Likoma in Nyasaland. The Likoma and Uganda cathedrals were, however, built by native Christians who could justify the existence of the imposing superstructures. But the number of Christians gained by the CMS at Mombasa or in the outlying areas was so small that it could not justify the existence of the cathedral.

On the highlands church buildings and estates were more the sign of the presence of the missionaries before the First World War than of the African converts they had gained. The CMS admitted in 1908, that their native Christians were comparatively few; about half of them were concentrated in Nairobi. But even here a majority had come from the coast with the railway. By the end of the decade the Church of Scotland frankly admitted that the pride of the mission was in the estate rather than in the number of Christians gained. They hoped that their estate would meet the expenses of running their Kikuyu Mission and would enable them to establish a chain of stations towards Mount Kenya: the station was to be self-supporting where possible by agricultural or industrial work, but where that was not possible it was to be supported from Kikuyu, with finances from the estate.

This was, however, a transitional period. The missions were able to establish firm bases in the highlands in which lived their converts, and out of which the gospel would spread once this transitional period was over. The bases became, in essence, mission houses and centres of Western civilisation and Christianity.

Between 1900 and 1914 the CSM and the CMS repeatedly reported opposition to their work and to the opening of new stations from Kikuyu elders. In 1913 the CSM reported that the main feature of the previous year was marked by a settled opposition in the form of resistance to the gospel and the rejection of medical treatment.[53] In 1914 the Kikuyu opposed the opening of out-stations. The CMS faced formidable opposition from Chief Karuri and the elders of Kabete and Karathimo who openly prohibited their people from having any contact with the CMS mission station.[54] At Ndia, in the Embu district, the opposition of the elders to the missions assumed even greater significance. Alarmed at the increasing number of their people visiting Embu Mission for medical treatment, the chiefs and head-men assembled together and issued an order that none of their people was to visit the hospital without permission. The chiefs feared that these people would settle there. By 1912 government officers working around Kikuyu were complaining that mission-aries had become a source of constant trouble because they had enticed young girls and young women to abandon their homes and live in the mission stations.[55]

From the very beginning the British Protestant missions had been a grave social problem to African society in Kenya. The missionaries had demanded that their converts throw away their beliefs, customs and traditions and accept, without question or qualification, a completely new way of life, social code and morals. In short, they demanded a revolution: 'a rejection of those very things that bound the tribe together from kings and chiefs down to the lowest and most insignificant individual, (into) one organic whole controlled by an iron-bound code of duties.'[56] The missionaries failed miserably to adjust their religion to the African milieu but proudly believed, for example, that their own form of marriage and burial, their theological approach, their narrow concept of a family and individualism were best for the Kikuyu, Akamba, Teita, Nyika, Pokomo and Moslem Swahili. It is no wonder, then, that they began to legislate for their converts from their Olympian western palaces in the midst of Africa, and regarded everything African as, at best, heathen. By 1915 the Church of Scotland had drawn up a code of rules against sins as a condition for baptism.[57] The CMS had ruled, for instance, that its agents would be dismissed from their services with the mission if they took part in native dancing.[58]

But perhaps the most serious problem was their interference with African customary marriage system. It was difficult for the Victorian-Edwardian missionaries to understand that no marriage in any African community could be solemnised without its component parts, namely, dancing and drinking. There was no better form through which they could express their joy other than in dancing which was always accompanied by drinking. So, when the missions required their converts to refrain from dancing and drinking they were, in fact, eroding marriage, initiation and circumcision ceremonies. Moreover, the missionaries failed to see anything good in polygamy, even though this was ingrained in the tribal social fabric, carried prestige and was of great social and economic significance in African society. The more male children a family had the stronger the family and the tribe became. As for female children, Kenyatta said: 'It was necessary to have a number of female children who could also render assistance by cultivating the land and looking after the general welfare of the tribe, while the men were fighting to defend their homesteads. Furthermore, the society cannot do without them for they are the salt of the earth....'[59] Only polygamy could meet all these demands. So when the missionaries demanded that their adherents cast away their wives, they were demanding a complete revolution, and an impossibility. But, more importantly, had the African men done so, it would have meant shunning the responsibility they bore to their wives, children, community and the whole tribe. They would have lost their prestige, economy and wealth. This they could not do and still belong to the tribe.

For the unmarried converts the missionaries ensured that the boys married Christian girls and vice versa. In the early days of their work at Mombasa the CMS did not find it difficult to arrange marriage for the single freed slaves, for the missionaries posed as their parents and so placed themselves in a position of tribal authority to choose wives and husbands for those under their care. In the twentieth century the missionaries could always ensure this by arranging marriages among those resident on the mission. Residence in mission stations, was therefore, one way through which the white missionaries could enforce monogamy, for they ensured that their adult converts had Christian wives from the mission house. Those who could not obey the wishes of the missionaries were thrown out of the mission houses. It is no wonder then that African parents refused to allow their children to live in the mission stations, and disowned those who were enticed away from their homes by the missions.

It is perhaps not necessary to narrate here that residents in the mission stations were subject to a discipline equal only to, if not surpassing, that found in military camps. In Mombasa we have seen how the missionaries practised brutality so that they might save the souls of their converts. The same process was repeated in the highlands but with perhaps less brutality. The *kiboko* was used sparingly in the twentieth century since the British official then supervising civil action made its use by the missions an offence. In the late nineties the CMS at Mombasa lamented the passing to the civil courts of their power to punish their converts. They admitted that all they could do was to try to restrain their converts from sin through moral persuasion.[60]

At Mombasa the two old Protestant missions had tried in vain to prevent toddy making and palm wine tapping, in the eighties and nineties. They had even tried to introduce tea-drinking instead. But the Africans were quick to discover that this could not fulfil the social function for which their own beer was brewed. On the highlands they also tried, with no success, to forbid their converts' drinking beer. The American Inland Mission had, by 1914, ruled that total abstinence was a necessary condition for baptism, and John Arthur, agreeing mistakenly with C. E. Hurlburt that beer-drinking among the Kikuyu was synonymous with drunkenness, sought permission from the Church of Scotland Central Committee to require total abstinence as a condition for baptism.[61] Since no such rule existed in the constitution of the Church of Scotland he could not do so without interfering with the constitution. The CSM therefore circumvented the constitution by placing drunkenness along with the list of sins which John Arthur had proscribed as a bar to baptism. This shows that the missionaries were prepared to go outside the boundaries of the Home Committees and Constitutions, or to evade them, to root out what they considered to be evil customs among the Africans. Most of the Africans considered it a joke since such customs were ingrained in the whole fabric of the tribe. They refused to abide by the rules, even when the civil authority at times joined the missions to curtail drunkenness, not because they felt it was necessary for salvation, but because they considered that it reduced the efficiency of the tribes' labour force.

It is difficult to assess the impact of the British Protestant missions and all missions in general on the villages and reserves since they were so violently opposed by the older generation. This opposition to the social forces of Christianity is a real measure of the strength of tribal culture. The elders and the older generation defended the tribe, and tried to prevent the social disintegration which they rightly believed would result if they allowed the missionaries to prevail. To be sure the elders had a vested interest in doing so because the missionaries threatened their own authority over the younger generation, but we need not overemphasise this point. It was not only because the missionaries attacked beer-drinking and dancing that the old and wise men of the tribe opposed them. Rather, it was because they were attacking the foundation of the tribe. The Rev. Harry Leakey wrote:

> It was easy to collect large audiences in those days. They could come in bands to a service as sight seeing to a show. They used to call the mission service by the same name as their musical dancers. But when at last it began to dawn upon them that more than mere listening was expected of them and that a change of life, which must of necessity mean a revolution in national customs was looked for by the missionary they became violently opposed to his teaching.[62]

In 1910 the missions and the British protectorate officials became concerned about the social disruption of the converts. It became quite clear to the missionaries that while they were condemning all the social and cultural values of the African tribes in the Protectorate as evil and heathen, they had not been able to provide alternatives acceptable and understandable to their few converts. It was not the discipline and immoral behaviour of the unconfirmed, as reported by Binns,[63] that the CMS were worried and concerned about, but that of the converts who, displaced from their tribal authority and codes and without firm footing in the ways of the white missionaries and western civilization, had become a social problem. The Bishop of Mobasa moved to remedy this, at least among the CMS adherents. The CMS conference meeting at Mombasa in 1912 responded and set up a small committee composed of the Bishop, Archdeacon Binns and George Wright, to approach the government to press for the formation of Christian Councils of Elders in Christian settlements, to exercise tribal laws similar to those exercised by *kiamas* (native tribunals) in the tribe.[64]

In perhaps quite a different way, the CMS was most probably responding to the Native Tribunals Rules of 1911 in which the government established councils of elders in accordance with traditional customs. It must be said at once that all the tribes of the Protectorate, and in this case the Pokomo, Nyika, Akamba, Taita and Kikuyu had traditional councils of elders who dispensed tribal laws and regulations. The Protectorate government did not, therefore, set up a novel tribal administrative authority. But in 1907 they, in their own colonial fashion, had legalised what John Middleton mistakenly calls '*informal*' councils of elders. The change was not so much in the tribunals themselves, rather it was in its personnel since from now on, the government made sure that it appointed those who would cooperate with them.

The CMS, perturbed at the social disintegration and lack of moral or civil codes among their converts, which the mission had brought about, sought therefore a duplication of the same councils in their own Christian settlements. In other words, they were asking the government to set up reserves for Christian converts with Christian councils of elders similar to those formed and recognised by the government in the native reserves, to enforce tribal law as prevailing in the nearest tribe and punishing offenders by fining them or otherwise as they would have been punished had they remained heathen. The CMS singled out one particular difficulty to drive home its case, which was most probably the concern of all missions. Binns remarked:

> It is felt by all of us that there is something wanting in our organisation, and the question has been brought before us many times as concerning our young people who fall into the sin of fornication, and it has often been said that amongst the heathen, for instance the Wagiryama, if a young fellow seduces a girl he is brought before the elders of the tribe and has to pay a fine amounting in some cases to the dowry which would have to be paid for the girl if she were married, whereas if a lad who professes Christianity is guilty of the same sin he is not punished at all: consequently, there is among those who profess Christianity a proportionately much larger number who

are guilty in this way as there is not the same amount of restraint as amongst the heathen.[65]

In the first half of the decade, the government had become aware of the social problems of the converts. Girouard wanted to set up inalienable native reserves in which chiefs and headmen would have definite powers and positions of authority within the tribe. The missionaries, on the other hand, demanded that these chiefs and elders should be denied authority over African Christian converts, hitherto members of the tribe, and that distinct local administrative units should be set up especially for their converts.[66] Girouard was unwilling to see Christian converts put into their own reserves, within the native reserves, and severed from their chiefs and headmen. But the general problem and position of the converts, as shown by the CMS and government concern, demanded a general review and thorough examination. In 1912 the governor set up a Native Converts' Committee to consider the position of the converts in the Kikuyu reserves. The committee was composed of the Provincial Commissioner for Ukamba, C. W. Hobley; District Commissioner, Fort Hall, G. A. Northcote: and Assistant District Commissioner, Kiambu, A. D. Dundas.[67]

The Native Converts Committee held discussions with Chiefs Kinyanjui, Matato, Mimi, Njiri and elders.[68] Representatives of the converts were drawn from both Protestant and Roman Catholic missions around Kikuyuland, but with a majority from missions centred in Kiambu. There were five from the Church of Scotland Mission, Kiambu, six from the French Mission, Kiambu, and two from the Italian Mission, Fort Hall.[69] The government deliberately excluded representatives of the white missionaries from the discussions for fear that they might prejudice the deliberations. The committee held the view that the question of the position of the converts in the native reserves was solely theirs, perhaps in consultation with their parents and the government. Hobley noted: 'One must not lose sight of the fact that the function of the missions is only a spiritual one and that they should not be allowed in any way to interfere with tribal organisation, laws of inheritance, etc.'[70]

The discussions centred on the touchy problems of land tenure, marriage, inheritance and tribal authority (kiama). From the deliberations emerged, above all, and much to the disappointment of the missionaries, unanimity among all the converts in their desire to retain identity with the Kikuyu tribe and to abide once again by the Kikuyu laws, customs and traditions. The converts' loud cry 'We wish to live with our fathers and not with the missionaries,'[71] would seem to indicate that the missionaries had made very little impact on them. For the time being the converts rejected, unequivocally, the wish of the missionaries that they live a life apart and detached from that of the traditional Kikuyu. They refused to be placed, as the missionaries were asking, under their own Christian Councils of Elders, but wanted to be under the jurisdiction of the *kiama*. They also refused to have any system of marriage other than that of the Kikuyu, and expressed the wish to abide by all the arrangements relating to courtship although the missionaries mistook the pre-marriage arrangements and the customary exchange of presents as 'dowry'.[72] Call it what they would, their converts would not depart from it.

Missionaries were presumptuous enough to claim to be guardians of children and widows of deceased converts, on the ground that they had arranged and paid dowry for the converts to fulfil tribal obligations before they got married.[73] So, they entertained the hope that the widows and children would remain in the mission and not pass into the hands of their pagan relatives, according to tribal custom. They had even hoped to control and have a share of any of their movable property. The converts, on their part, denounced and rejected at once any such claims by the missions, and quickly declared their desire to be inherited according to Kikuyu customs and traditions. In so doing the converts were, by implication, saying that their hearts, souls and bodies were with the tribe and not with the missionaries. Thus the missionaries had not succeeded in making them Christians and, as they had hoped, different from any genuine Kikuyu.

The missions failed to provide their converts with a lasting tenure which would have served as a great inducement for them to stay on the mission, even when they wavered about Christianity. Lasting land tenure on the mission estates was of particular importance to the converts since their residence there was considered, by the chiefs and Kikuyu elders, to be a bar to taking and owning land again in the reserves. Converts therefore invariably became landless once they left the mission as they could not retain their plots on the mission estates once they were outside. Such a position posed a serious dilemma, not only for them but also for the administration. Once the converts were given a choice, they preferred to remain on the reserve since owning land there did not entail the added demands made upon them on the mission land. Those whose land passed to the mission were in an even more serious position. Philip Karanja, representing the converts, said:

When a convert leaves the mission he is not allowed to retain his shamba on the mission land. [Converts] had nowhere to go to as many of the elders would not let them have land in the reserve. They are debarred from dancing in at ngomas and participating in other tribal observances.[74]

NOTES

1. Roland Oliver, *The Missionary Factor in East Africa* (London, 1952), p. 168.
2. William Price to Lang, May 18, 1889, G3 A5/06, CMS Archives, London.
3. *CMS Proceedings*, 1900/01, p. 116.
4. Oliver, pp. 169–170.
5. F. B. Welbourn and B. A. Ogot, *A Place to Feel at Home* (London, 1966), p. 21.
6. Kibwezi Jubilee Book, 1891–1948, typed manuscript in J. W. Arthur Papers, University of Edinburgh Library Archives, Edinburgh. (Cited hereafter as Arthur Papers, University of Edinburgh Archives.)
7. H. R. A. Philp, *A New Day in Kenya* (London, 1936), pp. 134–135.
8. *Ibid.*, pp. 57, 149.
9. Unnumbered Minute Book of the Foreign Missionary Committee of the United Methodist Church (Marylebone Road, London), p. 376. (Cited hereafter as FMC of UMC, London.) The United Methodist Free Church merged with the United Methodist Church in 1907.
10. Charles Eliot to Landsdowne, April 18, 1903, FO 2/712, Public Records Office. (Cited hereafter as PRO).
11. Joseph Kirsop, *Life of Robert Moss Ormeroid, Missionary to East Africa* (London, 1901), p. 127.
12. *Ibid.*
13. Charles N. E. Eliot, *The East Africa Protectorate* (London, 1905), p. 241.
14. *Ibid.*
15. H. R. Tate to Acting Chief Secretary, May 3, 1918, PC/CP/4/1/1, Kenya National Archives, Nairobi.
16. Kilifi Political Records, Vol. II, Annual Report 1910–1911, KFI 11, Kenya National Archives, Nairobi.

17. Kibwezi Jubilee Book 1891–1941, p. 7. Arthur Papers, University of Edinburgh Archives.
18. *Ibid.*, p. 8.
19. *Ibid.*, p. 9.
20. Thomas Watson to MacKinnon, January 27, 1899, MS 8016, 'East Africa Scottish Mission,' National Library of Scotland.
21. Watson to the Secretary, October 25, 1899, MS 8016, 'East Africa Scottish Mission,' National Library of Scotland and Kibwezi Jubilee Book 1891–1941, p. 14. Arthur Papers, University of Edinburgh Archives.
22. J. W. Arthur to Mclachlan, August 31, 1926, Arthur Papers, University of Edinburgh Archives.
23. Bishop W. G. Peel to Hatch, August 27, 1903, in file marked 'Letters to 1913,' Archbishop of East Africa Archives, Nairobi. (Cited hereafter as Bishop's Archives, Nairobi.)
24. *Ibid.*
25. Bishop Peel to Hatch, July 17, 1902, in file marked 'Letters to 1913,' Bishop's Archives, Nairobi.
26. Bishop Peel to Hatch, August 27, 1903, in file marked 'Letters to 1913,' Bishop's Archives, Nairobi.
27. W. S. McLachlan to Arthur, April 25, 1912, MS 7559, National Library of Scotland.
28. River Tana District Political Records, Vol. II, DC/TRD 3/2.
29. Dagoretti Political Record Book, Vol. II, 1902–1912, p. 6. KBU/76, Kenya National Archives, Nairobi.
30. Henry Scott to Mclachlan, September 29, 1909, MS 8016, National Library of Scotland.
31. Unnumbered Minute Book, FMC of UMC London.
32. Provincial Commissioner to Commissioner for Local Government, Lands and Settlement, March 18, 1913, Coast 2/549, Kenya National Archives, Nairobi.
33. Vincent Harlow, E. M. Chilver and Alison Smith, *History of East Africa*, Vol. II (Oxford, 1965), Appendix I, pp. 676–678.
34. Scott to Girouard, May 1, 1910, enclosure in Girouard to Secretary of State for Colonies, September 30, 1900, CO 533/90, PRO.
35. Peel to Girouard, October 19, 1910, enclosure in Girouard to Secretary of State for Colonies, September 30, 1900, CO 533/90, PRO.
36. *Ibid.*
37. S. Allegyer to Girouard, September 6, 1910, enclosure in Girouard to Secretary of State for Colonies, September 30, 1911, CO 533/90, PRO.
38. Bishop Peel to Baylis, November 14, 1914, G3 A5/019, CMS Archives, London.
39. Scott to Hobley, May 29, 1909, DC/MKS/IOA/I/6, Kenya National Archives, Nairobi.
40. Percy Girouard to Secretary of State for Colonies, August 14, 1911, CO 533/89, PRO.
41. Sir Frederick Jackson to Secretary of State for Colonies, October 22, 1909, CO 533/62, PRO.

42. Lord Crewe to Jackson, November 8, 1909, CO 533/63, PRO.
43. Secretariat Circulars, No. 33, April 16, 1914, DC/MKS, Kenya National Archives, Nairobi.
44. Girouard to Crewe, January 24, 1916, CO 533/71, PRO.
45. Girouard to Harcourt, June 11, 1911, CO 533/88, PRO.
46. *Ibid.*
47. J. J. Willis, 'Reunion,' undated typed manuscript, p. 1, Arthur Papers, University of Edinburgh.
48. *Ibid.*
49. *Ibid.*, p. 1.
50. *Ibid.*, pp. 1–2. The Bishop of Zanzibar's viewpoint is discussed by himself; see Frank Weston, *The Case Against Kikuyu: A Study in Vital Principles* (London, 1914).
51. *CMS Proceedings*, 1906/1907, p. 243.
52. Eugene Stock, *History of the Church Missionary Society*, 4 vols. (*London*, 1899–1916), IV, p. 77.
53. *Kikuyu News*, July-August, 1913, p. 21.
54. *CMS Proceedings*, 1911–1912, p. 48.
55. Handing over report, Dagoretti 1912–1913, KBU/76, p. 15.
56. Jomo Kenyatta, *Facing Mount Kenya* (London, 1938), p. 271.
57. Mclachlan to Arthur, November 16, 1916, MS 7572, National Library of Scotland.
58. Minutes of the British East Africa Mission, CMS in file marked 'Diocese of Mombasa—Cumulative Minutes,' Bishop's Archives, Nairobi.
59. Kenyatta, p. 175.
60. *Extracts, Annual Letters*, CMS, 1895, pp. 203–204.
61. McLachlan to Arthur, November 16, 1916, MS 7572, National Library of Scotland.
62. Harry Leakey to Baylis, May 17, 1910, G3 A5/–18, CMS Archives, London.
63. Binns to Provincial Commissioner, July 31, 1912, enclosure in Tate to Acting Chief Secretary, August 5, 1912, Coast 64/252, Kenya National Archives, Nairobi.
64. *Ibid.*
65. *Ibid.*
66. Bishop Peel to Baylis, November 14, 1910, G3 A5/018, CMS Archives, London.
67. Chief Secretary to Tate, March 14, 1912, Coast 64/252, Kenya National Archives, Nairobi.
68. Hobley to Chief Secretary, 'Précis of a Meeting held at Kiambu,' April 25 and 26, 1912, Coast 64/652, Kenya National Archives.
69. *Ibid.*
70. *Ibid.*
71. *Ibid.*
72. *Ibid.*
73. *Ibid.*
74. *Ibid.*

6

Missionary Attitudes and Actions Towards Forced Labour, Native Paramountcy and African Politics, 1919-1925

When the 1914–1918 war came, the Africans of Kenya were as much involved in it as anybody else. This was essentially a European war which they did not understand. However, many thousands of able-bodied Africans in Kenya were conscripted and saw service in Tanganyika, then German East Africa, mainly in the Carrier Corps.[1]

The war found the missionaries struggling to gain converts in the highlands. Likewise it found the settlers of Kenya struggling with the pioneering problems. As far as the missionaries were concerned, the opposition of the Africans to their work was more important than the coming war.

When conscription into the Carrier Corps was enforced, many African able-bodied men sought refuge, in the mission stations, where they were only too willing to become Christians. For a while the number of converts in the missions increased and the missionaries were happy with what they mistakenly believed was a positive response towards Christianity. However, they refrained from receiving any more escapees from conscription once they discovered the true reason why so many able-bodied African men wanted to become Christians.

In response to the British call for more carriers as the war effort became more intense, in 1917 the British Protestant missions formed the Mission Carrier Corps, better known as the Kikuyu Mission Volunteers.[2] Recruits came mainly from the Church of Scotland mission, the Church Missionary Society and the African

Inland Mission, the three Protestant missions already working in the highlands. Altogether they raised 1 750 volunteers and, commanded by J. W. Arthur of the CSM, they served for nine months in Southern Tanganyika, especially in Iringa area, where they occupied Muhanga and Boma Mzinga.

When the war ended in 1918, the African soldiers and carriers returned home to Kenya only to be affected by the post-war developments more adversely than any other British colonial people. Apart from war casualties which numbered 46 000, the famine and influenza epidemic which struck Kenya immediately after the war took an even higher toll. While British soldiers returning from the war were lavishly rewarded with Kenya's best land and with financial aid for its development, the Africans were robbed of their land for this purpose. In 1919 the settlers were rewarded with the beginning of representative government for having defended the empire and in the following year Kenya was changed from a protectorate to a colony. As will be detailed below, from 1919 the African peoples of Kenya were compelled to supply the settlers with labour and were relegated to an inferior status when they were required to carry an identification card, *the kipande*, which was the colonial government device for pinning down the Africans to working for European farmers.

The change in the status of the country was not merely a change of name. It meant, as Governor Northey announced, that the interests of the settlers and of Europeans in general would be paramount in the new colony. Henceforth the interests of the Africans would be subordinated to those of the Europeans.

The position of the missionaries on this policy is interesting, especially when their actions and the statements they made do not seem to tally with their proclaimed interest to act as trustees of the Africans. In this Chapter we will attempt to look into the policy and the attitude of the Protestant missions towards forced labour which the administration intended to implement, towards native paramountcy and towards militant African political associations which the Africans formed in response to that policy.

Addressing the Mission Council at Kikuyu in 1920, J. W. Arthur of the CSM foreshadowed the policy that the missions, at least the British Protestant ones, were to follow.

Kenya is to be one of the most important assets of the British

Empire. The missionaries are an integral part of the Colony, and must work with the Government and settlers for the good of the whole. We are in a particular sense the trustees of the native peoples and we must see that their interests are safeguarded and forwarded. . . . It is further impossible for us—nor would we wish to do so—to dissociate ourselves from the members of the British Empire and of the Kingdom of God from the political life of the country. . . . The other great force —settlers. Here there is no desire on our part to dissociate ourselves from their lives. . . . We can help the settler in many ways: supplying him with trained boys, clerks, artisans and hospital dressers etc. . . .[3]

However, the immediate problem facing the colonial administration immediately after the war was not the shortage of trained boys and artisans but of cheap labour for the development of the plantation economy. Shortage of labour began to be felt by the settlers during the first decade of the new century and it became acute during the war and immediately thereafter. A Labour Commission to look into the question was appointed in 1912–1913.[4] The commissioners, who included J. W. Arthur, heard a lot of evidence from which emerged two diverging views. All the settlers giving evidence unanimously advocated that native taxation should be increased to drive the native out of the Reserves to earn money. They also maintained that the Reserves should be reduced to the minimum.[5] This was the recommendation that the Labour Inquiry Board, appointed by the Governor Sir James Hayes Sadler, had made in 1908:

The land set aside for Native Reserves should be limited to the present requirements of the natives; the committee being of the opinion that the existence of unnecessarily extensive reserves is directly antagonistic to an adequate labour supply.[6]

Against the settlers were ranged administrative officials and missionaries. They spoke against both increase in taxation and reduction of the Reserves. Mr C. R. Lane, an administrative officer, stated that the latter step might assist the labour supply but would ruin the Reserves. C. W. Hobley, another administrative officer, maintained that there should be enough room for expansion so that there would be enough land to allow for the increase of population over three generations.[7]

Most of the missionaries were opposed to any step that would ruin the Reserves, and with them the African home and family. Most of them complained of the crude conditions to which the Africans, as labourers, were subjected, and also condemned the brutality of the employers. Ruffel Barlow of the CSM put forward a representative view of most missionaries:

As regards Kenya province, one doubts whether the number of natives leaving it to go to work could very well be increased. The maximum supply of labour has been obtained for some time back by means of a press-gang system put into force by the chiefs. The usual argument that one meets when urging that the native needs time to attend to his own affairs is that the male native while at home does not work, but roams about watching his women slave for him. This is an erroneous idea.[8]

Settlers had argued for compulsion on the mistaken ground that the African male was lazy, and spent most of his time getting drunk. The settlers, however, were entirely ignorant of the division of labour inherent in African society. The only time that the settlers ever saw the Africans at leisure was probably either immediately after the harvest when they were enjoying the fruits of their toil, or during the rainy season, when they had long finished breaking the ground up and the women had also finished putting the seeds into the ground. But, even at this time, the Africans had their homes to attend to and huts to repair or to put up new ones.

The Anti-Slavery and Aborigines' Protection Society wrote a long memorandum to the Colonial Office, challenging the view of the settlers that it was the duty of the government to provide labour for industrial development.[9] It reiterated, more strongly than the commission had done, that any form of administrative recruitment was bound to lead to compulsion and stressed that forced labour for private profit was slavery.[10] However, it pointed out that the best form of incentive to a steady flow of labour was not compulsion by administrative decree but a good employer, good treatment and better conditions of services. It was the lack of confidence in the employers and in government protection, the society maintained, that caused a serious shortage of labour.

The commissioners were opposed to increasing direct African taxation but they were silent on whether or not the reserves should be further reduced to force people to go out to work for private farms.

During the war years, Kenya government officials had to help settlers to get labour, without which the settler-based economy of Kenya faced ruin. They had devised various means among which were direct recruitment and a press-gang system. The use of these methods implied compulsion and clearly this was disguised forced labour not only for public works but for private employers. Certainly from 1917 through 1918, the official view was that labour must be forthcoming for private employers. With the shortage of labour, due to the government's intensive conscription to the carriers, officials often forced young boys to go out to work, not only on public duties but also for settlers. There were complaints from the missions (the CSM at Tumutumu is a case in point) that the government was forcing boys to go out to work.[11]

After about 1917, however, some of the missionaries began to support forced labour for the development of the plantation economy of Kenya. They began to identify their interest with that of the administration and of the settlers. For as they seemed to have surmounted the initial period of African opposition to their work which had been made possible only with the support of the administration, they became even more arrogantly convinced of the 'white man's burden'. And like the settlers, they went ahead with the mission to build the British Empire in Kenya with unequalled enthusiasm and determination.

To be sure Arthur had argued that the missions were henceforth to become an arm of the colonial administration as members of the British Empire. On the more specific question of the role of the African peoples in the economic development of the colony, another missionary, Horace Philp, maintained that the Africans had to provide the labour force required for the development of the colony and stressed that it was the duty of the government to ensure that such a labour force would be forthcoming.

I believe it criminal of the government to allow unsound economic development, e.g. to attract settlers here and give them land and not to see that there is an adequate labour supply for their needs. If this happens and the settlers rise up in arms against the Government, and is the Government not to blame?[12]

Philp's view came to dominate missionary thinking and attitudes when the administration adopted the policy of forced African labour after the war. How much such a policy was influenced by this attitude is not significant. Rather it is their support of it.

At the end of the war many of the settlers who had been fighting the Germans in Tanganyika returned home to Kenya. In 1919 they were joined by a larger wave of settlers from England whom the British government re-settled in Kenya under the newly formed Ex-Soldiers' Settlement Scheme. Their coming increased the problem of the labour force which was already critical. Both the war and the post-war diseases and epidemics had drastically reduced the population of the Reserves. Nevertheless the settlers opened their campaign for a government policy of African forced labour. They found a useful ally in the new governor, Edward Northey, an ex-general, who in 1919 announced to the Convention of Associations, a political association of White Settlers, that he would introduce legislation to make the current policy of encouraging labour effective.[13] His Chief Native Commissioner followed this up with the Labour Circular No. 1 of October 23.[14] Essentially, the Labour Circular No. 1 instructed all government officials, chiefs and headmen, to recruit labour for private employers. The two relevant clauses in the circular state that:

all Government officials in charge of Native areas must exercise every possible lawful influence to induce able-bodied male natives to go out into the labour field. Where farms are situated in the vicinity of a native area, women and children should be encouraged to go out for such labour as they can perform.... Native Chiefs and Elders must at all times render all possible lawful assistance on the foregoing lines....[15]

The Bishops of Mombasa and of Uganda, R. S. Heywood, J. J. Willis, and the head of the CSM, J. W. Arthur, immediately responded to the Labour Circular. In what became popularly known as the Bishops' Memorandum they criticised, in detail, every item in it.[16] While the bishops recognised, clearly, that the government memorandum introduced 'compulsory labour'[17] they stated that they were not concerned whether it was a bad thing or a good thing.[18]

In a confidential letter to Governor Northey, Arthur pointed out that the bishops were not opposed to his policy, only to its administration.

With regard to dances, idleness, and drunkenness, naturally, we are at one with you in the desire to see these stopped and the native becoming a useful industrious citizen of the country. Our criticism, of course, is set at, not attacking the policy, but the best way to obtain the result. We all know the abuses in the Native Reserve, when the chiefs get men to go out to work, we want the men to work, and after much consideration, think that compulsory labour, with proper safeguards, will be better for the country and the native; in spite of the arguments against it, of the criticism that may be levelled at us, we would prefer to see such compulsion. Believing so, we considered it was up to us to candidly say so, and, if compulsory labour is adopted, then you, Sir, know our position with regard to it.

Again with regard to the women and children we have no objection either to such going out voluntarily, but we were very afraid lest the chiefs, with considerable power and the support of Government behind them, should abuse that power. We do agree on the main principles. . . .[19]

The bishops took particular exception to the wide powers that the circular gave to the chiefs who they believed would abuse them. The bishops would have preferred these powers to be given to the British officials.[20]

There is little doubt that, in their excessive zeal to please the British officials, who were after all their employers, the chiefs and elders often carried their power to the extreme. Missionaries had reported that the chiefs were cruel in forcing the people to work, and cases of bribery and corruption resulting from forced labour were not unusual. Africans giving evidence to the Labour Commission had complained of the pressure they suffered under native officials to leave the villages and work for wages elsewhere. Thuku stated that the chastity of girls had been abused, though

123

he was not clear whether the chiefs or the settlers were to blame.

Fundamentally, however, these abuses were a result of the policy of forced labour which the missionaries were supporting. It is difficult to see how the missionaries could accept the broad lines of the policy while objecting to its repercussions. Indeed their support for forced labour seemed to stem from their conviction that they were doing the right thing for the empire and for the natives, and for this reason they were prepared to ignore any criticisms. Hence Arthur could write, 'In spite of the arguments against it, of the criticisms that may be levelled at us, we would prefer to see such compulsion'.[21]

Our evidence from the confidential communication between Arthur and the governor on November 5 immediately after the Bishops' Memorandum was issued, shows that the heads of the two British Protestant missions in Kenya, or their representatives, had approved of the principles of this policy.[22] The papers containing the correspondence were only made available after the death of J. W. Arthur in 1952 when his wife generously gave them to the University of Edinburgh and allowed researchers to make use of them. The same is true of Kenya Archives which have been reorganised after independence. In his letter Arthur had reiterated the missionaries' claim that compulsory labour was better for the country and for the natives, and providing that chiefs and headmen were not made the agency for recruitment, such a policy was sound. Indeed the governor had in confidential correspondence persuaded Arthur and with him the other Protestant heads of the moral force of the measure to the Africans. He had reiterated that behind it was his concern for the prosperity of the country and for the natives.[23] He had maintained, though without any proof, that forced African labour would stop idleness and drunkenness which was so rife among the African population of Kenya.[24] Certainly nothing could be farther from the truth, for the governor's real motive was to make the African serve the economic interests of the settlers. The high moral tone of the governor's utterance obviously found enthusiastic support in the missionaries who with their Victorian moral righteousness were keen to inculcate such values in the Africans. In affirmation Arthur maintained that the work of the missions was based on the 'belief that every native ought to work and that work was a necessary part of Christianity. To Christianise natives to educate

124

them and to make them work were complementary principles'.[25]

Arthur, however, utterly failed to recognise that it was, conversely, unchristian to force some to work for the benefit of others, and that the policy he was so religiously supporting was aimed at exploiting the labour of the Africans for the benefit of the settlers and of Britain. Outside Kenya very serious criticisms were expressed against the bishops' support for the policy. Bishop Frank of Zanzibar wrote:

> And how the Bishops of Mombasa and Uganda have played traitors! It is too horrible for words and few people get red-hot against it. I am heart-sick with Christian institutions—though you find Christ riding on such asses. My inner mind is to cut myself off from the British, and throw in my lot entirely with the Bantu.[26]

In a letter to the African Secretary at Salisbury Square the Rev. Percy Waller called for CMS intervention on the issue and sarcastically reported that 'the good missionaries had accepted the policy with safeguards ... but they had in that way accepted the principle of forced labour for private behoof.'[27] As for the forced labour controversy, enlightened missionaries and Oldham in particular saw that it barely concealed the British colonial policy of subordinating the interests of the African *peoples* of Kenya to the economic interests of the white settlers.[28] Indeed Governor Northey had expressly stated it, as Commissioner Elliot before him had done at the beginning of the new century. There was therefore little doubt of this being the British policy as long as Kenya remained a British colony.

In response to missionary criticisms that chiefs would abuse their powers, if they were made agents of recruiting labour, Governor Northey instructed his administrative officials to see that chiefs and headmen did not do so. Mainly through the efforts of Oldham and missionary societies in Britain the Colonial office ruled against compulsory labour for private employers in Kenya in 1921.[29] But even before this the colonial administration had brought in legislation which reduced the Africans to a labour-exporting peasantry. There was already the *kipande* system referred to earlier, and the government moved to double African direct taxation, from eight shillings to sixteen in 1920. This was certainly an indirect way of forcing the Africans to sell their labour for wages. Although in the early period it was possible for some Africans to sell their animals and their surplus crops for money to pay tax,[30] it became increasingly difficult for them to do so as their population grew while the size of the Reserves diminished. So the Africans had to sell their labour-power to get the money and the labour problem seemed to have been solved even without the labour laws. Norman Leys confirmed that 'direct taxation of the poorest people in the colony, up to the limit of endurance, and a Registration Ordinance that makes evasion of wage earning impossible seem to have solved the labour problem in Kenya!'[31]

Oldham, however, had not succeeded in getting the Colonial Office to agree to the declaration of native policy he had pressed for. Only in 1923 did the Colonial Office issue a policy statement embodying the paramountcy of African interests in Kenya.[32] The Devonshire Declaration which declared that primarily Kenya is an African country came as the Indians were then demanding equal rights with whites particularly equal franchise, unrestricted immigration and the opening of the highlands to them. They denied the Indians equal rights using the Declaration as an excuse and with regards to the paramountcy in the Africans interests which the Declaration enumerated, they simply ignored it. That is why the declaration remained a paper document until the bloody Mau Mau uprising of 1952–1956 forced the colonial administration to effect the policy which culminated in African rule in 1963.

In 1922 it looked as if the Colonial Office would concede the Indians most of their claims, as the Wood-Winterton Committee which it had appointed to study the question then recommended for a common electoral roll based on a non-discriminatory property and educational test, and unrestricted immigration.[33] The settlers could not agree to such a whittling away of their supremacy and they raised a hue and cry against it. So effective were their protests that the Colonial Office suspended the implementation of the recommendations indefinitely and called for a conference of the representatives of settlers and Indians in London the following year. Ironically, the Africans whose interests at the conference were pawned for those of the whites were represented by J. W. Arthur.[34]

The British Protestant missions were deeply involved in the

issue. Both the Europeans and the Africans with whom they had special interests, would be affected by the outcome one way or the other. Common sense alone dictated that it could certainly have been in their best interests if such an outcome were in favour of the Europeans. Most of them supported the cause of the settlers.[35] Almost all of them were invited by the settlers as a body either through the alliance or individually, as Europeans. Although the Alliance had turned down the invitation to become a member of the Convention of Associations, it regularly sent its representative. In the convention its representative could not vote but participated fully in the deliberations. Arthur said:

> the presence of missionaries in the past has been appreciated by the Convention, decisions have been influenced ... we have supported the Europeans in the general policy which has been taken up for the sake of the Africans but have urged that we could not come out into the open on the matter without complicating the position not only of Missions in India but of the whole cause of Christianity there.[36]

McGregor Ross, then the Director of Public works, noted that the missionaries appeared and spoke at anti-Indian meetings and some, he said, wrote when they could not appear.[37] He said, 'There is little to be said for the missionaries. They have shown only too much eagerness to allow themselves to be stampeded by the fatuous "Fascists"!'[38]

Clearly a majority of the resident missionaries were in support of maintaining white supremacy in Kenya, and to do so they used the African interest to gain it. Most of them knew that conceding the Indian equality with the European would jeopardise the *status quo* since they would swamp Europeans in almost every walk of life in the colony by sheer weight of numbers.

Representing African interests, R. S. Heywood maintained that unrestricted immigration could bring into Kenya the type of Indians whose interests would be directly against those of the Africans for they would take up lower industrial and electrical jobs that were directly open to the Africans.[39]

In the Indian controversy, Oldham saw the opportunity to press the Colonial Office to a declaration of native policy in Kenya. He believed that the settlers of Kenya would agree to a principle of the paramountcy of African interests rather than to equality with the Indians as long as they could be made trustees of these interests. After all, all the participants realised that they could win their case only if they accepted the principle of trusteeship and it was on this understanding that the settlers and the missionaries accepted the Devonshire Declaration.

In fairness to the resident missionaries we must point out that had they refrained from publicly criticising the administrative aspects of the forced labour policy, it might not have received the attention it did outside Kenya. But whether there would have been any difference in the policy afterwards pursued by the administration is very doubtful. For in Kenya theory became radically different from practice between 1920 and 1956. And it must also be conceded that by protecting the Africans from the abuses of the chiefs and headmen the missionaries were, according to what they firmly believed, fulfilling their duty as trustees of the Africans. But the issue here is that of forced labour which they endorsed in principle. Their attitude clearly proved that they were prepared to sacrifice the interests of the Africans to those of Europeans and of the empire.

The Indian question was certainly a side issue as far as the Africans were concerned for what was at stake here was white supremacy in Kenya. Missionaries inevitably sided with the settlers to argue the case of white supremacy and pawned African interest to maintain the *status quo*. The labour question, however, showed the Africans that they could not trust the missionaries to speak on their behalf. Neither the missionaries, nor the Indians, not to mention the settlers, were at all interested in the paramountcy of African interests in Kenya.

In the wave of further alienation of land under 'the post World War I Ex-Soldiers' Settlement Scheme the security of African land was seriously threatened. The Masai had already lost their land to the railway line between 1904 and 1911 and so too had the Nandi and the Kikuyu. Evidently it became clear to them that they would be even more seriously affected by the second wave of rape. As a result the chiefs and some headmen formed the Kikuyu Association in 1920 to fight against further alienation of their land and for its security.[40] Mainly rural-oriented, it became primarily interested in the problems of rural Kikuyu. From its inception it worked within the premises of the colonial administration. Partly because a majority of its members were chiefs and head-men, the association broadly accepted the premise of colonial rule. As such it was not interested in changing the *status quo* in colonial Kenya but in seeking improvement first for its members and secondly for the Kikuyu in general within it. This is clearly demonstrated by the desire to help the administration in the collection of taxes and to improve the welfare of chiefs and head-men which the Association had expressed to the colonial administration in one of its early representations to the government.[41]

Perhaps its most radical demand was its protest in the first half of 1921 against the European campaign to have African wages in Kenya reduced by one third. In this the association was at one with the Young Kikuyu Association which Harry Thuku had proposed during the first week of June that year. But in most other things the two associations came to be ranged against one another. The attitude and the actions of the missionaries towards these two African associations, which we shall examine, spectacularly reveal the kinds of African politics they were prepared to support. It was largely the result of such attitudes that the missionaries came into conflict with progressive Africans in Kikuyu-land.

In June 1921, in the midst of the Kikuyu Associations' protest against the European campaign to have African wages reduced, the missionaries persuaded the administration to meet its representatives in an attempt to alleviate the situation which was already becoming extremely serious. Furthermore, one of them, a certain A. R. Barlow of the CSM, helped the Association to draw up a petition which was finally presented to the gathering at Dagoretti on 24 June which consisted of government officials, representatives of the association, of the missionaries and, unfortunately for the Kikuyu Association and the missionaries, of the Young Kikuyu Association. The petition demanded mainly the elevation of the status of the chiefs and headmen and only very generally the redressing of the grievances of the Kikuyu.[42] It thus diverted interest from the questions currently at issue. McGregor Ross commented:

A meeting of greater importance than most of the participants can have recognised at the time took place on June 24, 1921. Senior government officials were there from Narobi, District

E*

Officers, missionaries, Kikuyu chiefs and attendants, natives in red paint, mission boys and members of the Young Kikuyu Association in imported clothing—the old order and the new, in the native world; the government insistent upon respect for the recognised (and salaried) chiefs and headmen, younger men, acting in combination, thrusting themselves in between the paid chiefs and the government and claiming the attention which organisation always elicits.

The young men acted and spoke with a composure and self-confidence that grated upon the paid chiefs. They had attended mission schools for the sake of getting some education. Under the glib classification of the average white immigrant, they were 'mission boys'. To the missionaries many of them were known 'failures', who had responded little or not at all to mission influence but had only snatched the coveted boon of education, which the missions offered free and had then decamped with it. To the missionaries (as a body) they were an object of suspicion tinged with resentment. To the government they were a probable source of embarrasment. To the paid chiefs they were anathema. Nobody wanted them or to meet them, and here they were forcing a hearing.[43]

The meeting at Dagoretti marked the beginning of a new era in African politics as it led to an increased identification of the missionaries with the affairs of the Kikuyu Association and, much more seriously, the enstrangement of relations between them and the younger generation of Africans, many of whom were mission trainees. It was they who dominated the deliberations of the Dagoretti meeting, and it was mainly through the efforts of Harry Thuku of the proposed Young Kikuyu Association that their petition, rather than that of the Kikuyu Association, got publicised outside Kenya. For immediately thereafter Thuku wrote to the Colonial Secretary in London and drew his attention to the grievances of forced labour, the *Kipande* system, the reduction in wages, increase in taxation and the alienation of land under which the Africans were suffering, an action which cost him his job as government telephonist.[44] But this gave him the opportunity to work full-time in the Association and to embark on a marathon campaign for membership among the rural Kikuyu where he drew a large following. To widen the scope of his action and to elicit support outside Kikuyu land he toured Kavirondo and Ukambani.

As Thuku toured the rural areas of Kikuyu, missionaries witnessed with alarm the large following he drew wherever he went. His speeches then became positively violent and the missionaries and Europeans directly became his object of attack. McGregor Ross confirmed this, writing that 'as Thuku went towards Fort Hall a distinct anti-European note began to appear'.[45] By early 1922 the missionaries were excitedly reporting that a rebellion was imminent and they called for steps to be taken to restrain the Young Kikuyu Association and its activities.[46]

The missionaries and the Kikuyu Association burst into a furore over Thuku's unprecedented action, from which they dissociated themselves. Furthermore the attitude of the missionaries towards the Young Kikuyu Association was seriously hardened by Thuku's stand aginst them and the Europeans. At its first meeting held in Nairobi on July 10, which was attended by 2 000 people, the Young Kikuyu Association demonstrated its radicalism in demanding that the franchise be extended to all Africans of Kenya. And on the Indian question previously referred to, it resolved that the presence of Indians in Kenya was not, as the missionaries had argued, prejudicial to the advancement of the Africans.[47]

The Young Kikuyu Association was not the sort of African political association which the missionaries could entertain. For one thing it ignored altogether the intermediary role of the missionaries, like Handley Hooper of the CMS saw in the anti-behalf of the Africans of Kenya. This implied a lack of confidence both in them and in their work. Furthermore the association was demanding a share in the running of their country—a step which the missionaries firmly believed was premature.

Most of the missionaries wrongly believed that the Kenya Indians were behind Thuku and his movement. In March 1922, J. Arthur, Handley Hooper and Harry Leakey had reported that the Indians were behind him; they even said the Indians were using him for their own ends. Harry Leakey said that Thuku had all the dissatisfied Indian community and their money behind him. —'He goes up Fort Hall district in a magnificent car.'[48] Some missionaries, like Handley Hooper of the CMS saw in the anti-missionary movement the approaching end of the work of the missions in Kikuyu and with it, of course, Christian influence. Hooper wrote:

> In this district the future of mission work trembles in the balance. Harry Thuku, mouthpiece of a clever Indian lawyer, is playing a very hazardous game. He has created tremendous enthusiasm, not only in Kikuyu but Kavirondo and most Mohammedans as well as Christians ... a big element of the Christian community, the mystical section, are seeing in him a deliverer of the prophetic type, and religious fervour is contributing to his popularity.[49]

The anti-missionary nature of the movement, the majority of whose members were adherents of the missions, or had passed through them, was a great blow to the missionaries. If they had been wiser and more imaginative, they would have paused to take stock of their work and of their role. Thuku had lumped the missionaries and settlers together, and accused the missionaries of being the agents of the settlers.

Certainly such accusations were not without foundation. For one thing it could be shown through their actions that the missionaries served as an arm of the colonial administration even though they generally believed they constituted a separate power block. For they had not only supported the labour laws but their educational policy during this time was based on raising obedient labourers for the settlers and for themselves also. Although socially they were despised by most of the settlers politically they did mix with them. The missionaries attended political meetings of the settlers and, as in the India question, supported their objectives. And we have already mentioned that the missions also held land and cried for cheap labour.[50] Certainly this association between them emphasised their similarities as kith and kin rather than any differences they might have had.

Writing as recently as 1965 James Ngugi has said:

> Take Siriana Mission for example, the men of god came peacefully. They were given a place. Now see what has happened. They invited their brothers to come and take the land. Our country is invaded.[51]

The missionaries therefore strove to stifle the Young Kikuyu

Association. First, they tried to influence the movement in an attempt to play down the grievances it was articulating and, according to J. W. Arthur, 'to get them out of the hands of these Indian extremists who are merely using them for their own ends'.[52] As already seen, in so doing they helped to popularise the Young Kikuyu Association. Secondly the missionaries, having failed to gain an influence in Thuku's movement, worked directly but secretly to undermine it. It was at Weithaga CMS station that the CMS hatched a plot to do so.[53] It secretly manoeuvered with the officials of YKA, who were CMS Christians, to bring the movement into the open. Already the CMS was alarmed at the popularity of the movement among their Christians. From Weithaga CMS stations, Thuku drew an excessively large following second only to the crowd he drew at Fort Hall. These were not interested spectators but active members of the YKA. The CMS, in collaboration with its leaders at Weithaga, gathered the names of the YKA leaders and obtained sworn affidavits from them to persuade the government to order the early arrest of Thuku and the leading officials of the association.[54] The Weithaga CMS log book record for 1922 clearly shows this.[55] Unfortunately the names of the CMS Christians at Weithaga who were YKA officials are not recorded. Probably those who gave the information to the CMS missionaries were not aware of their sinister motives or otherwise they would not have co-operated with them.

Harry Thuku was arrested on March 15, 1922 because of a speech he had made at Weithaga the previous month.[56] Evidently the mission there had been responsible for his early arrest although it was inevitable sooner or later. Upon his arrest, thousands of his followers gathered around the police lines at Nairobi where he was detained. The events which led to the firing on the demonstrators then have not been fully and justifiably explained.

Oral evidence of the events is also difficult to obtain, due, no doubt, to the tension that had mounted before the firing opened and the panic which resulted. There is little doubt however, that the government was to blame for the mobilisation of the police and the army to deal with unarmed and peaceful demonstrators. The demonstrators did not get out of hand nor, as Harry Leakey subsequently confirmed, had they attempted to molest Europeans.[60] It is true that the demonstrators were many but this should have been expected in view of the seriousness of the situation and the intensity of feeling among the Africans. Altogether, twenty-five Africans were shot dead. Harry Thuku was deported to Kismayu until 1925 when he was removed to Marsabit. Two others, George Mugekenye and Waiyango were deported to the coast province.[58] However, the colonial government was forced to make some concessions and immediately thereafter moved to reduce the hut tax to twelve shillings, while it also forbade labour for women and children and immediately withdrew the one-third reduction in African wages.[59]

With the deportation of the YKA leaders came the proscription of the association which the missions had struggled to effect. African political activity did not die, however, but went underground where the Kikuyu began to organise secretly. The rank and file was not cowed for they still continued to express their ferment through political songs and dances, both of which proved to be powerful weapons of political expression and mobilisation. These songs and dances continued to attack chiefs as stooges of the administration as they also attacked the missionaries and settlers. On the advice of J. W. Arthur, the government imposed a ban on the songs and dances also,[60] much to the relief of the missionaries. On the surface at least, militant political activity among the Kikuyu was silenced, only to revive in 1925 with the formation of the Kikuyu Central Association.

The Kikuyu Association, on the other hand, was typical of the local political associations that most of the British Protestant missionaries in Kenya enthusiastically supported if not helped to organise. According to Handley Hooper of CMS Kahuhia such associations, without being official bodies, would work with the knowledge of the government to serve as a safety valve for African grievances.[61] If this were so the missionaries were obviously not interested in bringing about a radical change of the *status quo* or an immediate redress of the social, economic and political grievances of the Africans but only in bottling up their grievances.

In 1922, Harry Leakey was able to report that the Kikuyu Association was absolutely loyal, and that it had denounced Thuku and his movement.[62] Harry Leakey actually referred to the conservative Kikuyu Association as 'our' Kikuyu Association, which clearly shows that it was more a missionary association than an African one. Chief Koinange, Josiah and Philipo Karanja, the leaders of the association, toured the rural areas of Kikuyu with the District Commissioner to popularise their association and at the same time to discredit the YKA.[63] Harry Thuku returned the volley with unrivalled vehemence and attacked the chiefs as stooges of the missionaries and the administration. Leakey confirmed this, writing that '(Thuku) had issued so many scurrilous leaflets in Kiswahili; one, slanging Koinange and Josiah for refusing him, another against Simeon Kalume, our native pastor, others against missions generally'.[64]

In Kikuyu-land however, the missionaries did not succeed in diverting the Kikuyu from militant politics; nor did they succeed in emasculating the YKA or its successor, the Kikuyu Central Association. On the contrary, the missionaries' hostility to the YKA helped to stampede it into unprecedented popularity, while the Kikuyu Association, which they supported, never became popular.

In Nyanza province, however, the missions, particularly the CMS, succeeded in domesticating the mission graduates of the area who were likely leaders of militant African politics. In 1922 was formed the Young Kavirondo Association whose platform and programme of action was similar to that of the Young Kikuyu Association. At the meeting called at Lundha at which the association was launched feelings ran high and an open confrontation with the police would have led to a crisis had the police not withdrawn. The meeting passed far-reaching resolutions, the most important of which were against heavy taxes, compulsory labour and the conversion of the protectorate into a Crown colony. Oginga Odinga has said:

The great Lundha meeting which launched the Young Kavirondo Association and from which the Government had been excluded took place two days before Christmas in 1921. Nyanza was throbbing with tension and it was apparent that the government had been taken completely unawares. In February Luo people all over Nyanza held a giant Baraza, at Nyahera, not far from Kisumu. The meeting started at eight in the morning and went on until eight at night, and the people expounded on their ten points. Once again the people com-

135

plained about the change from Protectorate to Colony, about the high rate of hut and poll tax, about forced labour.[65]

In 1923 the CMS managed to divert the Young Kavirondo Association from militant political issues similar to those the Young Kikuyu Association articulated and which had led to the clash with the government in 1922. Instead Archdeacon Owen converted it into the Kavirondo Tax-payers' Welfare Association. Based on closest co-operation with the government, it became a welfare association of tax-payers and Owen became its first president, while leading government officials of the area became vice-presidents.[66] As such it never could articulate the political grievances of the people of the area and Oginga Odinga says 'the people never got the political rights or the association that they had demanded'.[67]

In fairness to Owen we must point out that he helped to prevent a recurrence of the incident which took place in Nairobi in Nyanza Province. Furthermore he was not always at one with the administration as he often clashed with it when his demands, though by no means radical, seemed a little ahead of government strategies. Certainly enthusiasts of the mission's role in Kenya would argue with some truth that the missionaries knew politics and Owen like the rest was operating with that understanding. As already said there seems little doubt to the author that they always fought for their kith and kin. In Nyanza they certainly were successful in diverting Africans from militant politics; in Kikuyu area their success was less.

Meanwhile the colonial administration accepted the claim of the missionaries to represent African interests in the colonial legislature. In 1924, much against African protest against the claim of the missionaries to speak for and represent African interests, J. W. Arthur was appointed to Kenya Legislative Council to represent the interest of the Africans. He was also appointed to the Executive Council of the colony. African protest against this paternalism began to be voiced during the Harry Thuku movement. Thuku maintained that only educated Africans would genuinely represent African interests. In 1930 Jomo Kenyatta, Secretary of the KCA, expressed the same view and further condemned the missionary representative for having 'failed to advance or to support African interests.[68] In spite of these protests, the colonial administration continued to appoint missionaries to the Legislative Council to represent African interests. Indeed the number of Europeans to represent African interests in the legislature was raised to two in 1934. Henceforth two Europeans, most of whom were missionaries, exercised this role till 1944. Then the first African, Eliud Mathu, was appointed to the legislature to replace one of them.

NOTES

1. Donald Savage and Forbes Munro, 'Carrier Corps Recruitment in the British East African Protectorate,' in *Journal of African History*, Vol. VII, No. 2, pp. 313–342.
2. J. W. Arthur, 'Kikuyu Mission Volunteer Corps, 1917–1918,' in J. W. Arthur Papers, University of Edinburgh Library Archives, Edinburgh. (Cited hereafter as Arthur Papers, University of Edinburgh Archives).
3. J. W. Arthur to Mclachlan, October 5, 1920, Arthur Papers, University of Edinburgh Archives.
4. Report of the Native Labour Commission, 1912–1913 (Nairobi, 1913).
5. Report of the Native Labour Commission, 1912–1913 (Nairobi, 1913), Vol. III, Minutes of Evidence.
6. McGregor W. Ross, *Kenya from Within* (London, 1927), p. 92.
7. Report of the Native Labour Commission, 1912–1913 (Nairobi, 1913), Minutes of Evidence.
8. *Kikuyu News*, September 15, 1913, pp. 20–21.
9. John Harris to Harcourt, June 11, 1914, C.O. 533/148, Public Records Office. (Cited hereafter as PRO).
10. *Ibid*.
11. Kenya Province, Annual Report, 1917–1918, PC/CP 4/1/1. Kenya National Archives. (Cited hereafter as Nairobi Archives).
12. Horace Philp, 'Memorandum to the Government,' Appendix in Kenya Province Annual Report, 1916–1917. PC/CP 4/1/1, Nairobi Archives.
13. Raymond Buell, *The Native Problems in Africa*, 2 vols. (New York, 1928), Vol. 1, p. 332. (Cited thereon).
14. McGregor W. Ross, *Kenya from Within* (London, 1927), p. 103–5 cited therein.
15. *Ibid*.
16. The Bishops' Memorandum, 'Native Labour,' in file marked 'Correspondence with Chief Native Commissioner, 1918–1939,' Archives of the Archbishop of East Africa, CMS Nairobi. (Cited hereafter as Bishop's Archives, CMS, Nairobi).
17. *Ibid*.
18. *Ibid*.
19. Arthur to Edward Northey, November 5, 1919 (confidential) Arthur Papers, Edinburgh University Archives.

20. *Ibid.*
21. *Ibid.*
22. *Ibid.*
23. Northey to Arthur, November 5, 1919, Arthur Papers, University of Edinburgh Archives.
24. *Ibid.*
25. Arthur to Oldham, May 20, 1920, IMC Archives, London.
26. Maynard Smith, *Frank Bishop of Zanzibar 1871–1924* (SPCK) 1926, p. 251.
27. Percy Waller to Manley, not dated, Correspondence of J. H. Oldham, IMC Archives, London.
28. Oldham to Bishop of Zanzibar, April 14, 1921. Correspondence of J. H. Oldham, IMC Archives, London.
29. Despatch to the Officer Administering the Government of Kenya relating to Native Labour, September 5, 1921, Cmd. 1509.
30. For this see the author's article 'The Giriama War 1914–1915' in B. Ogot (ed) *War and Society in Africa* (EAPH, forthcoming).
31. Norman Leys, Kenya, 2nd ed. (London, 1925), p. 195.
32. Indians in Kenya, 1923, Cmd. 1922 p. 9–10.
33. Buell, I. p. 291–94.
34. Arthur to Mclachlan, March 8, 1923, Arthur Papers, University of Edinburgh Archives.
35. *Ibid.*
36. *Ibid.*
37. McGregor Ross to Oldham, April 6, 1923, Correspondence of J. H. Oldham, IMC Archives, London.
38. *Ibid.*
39. R. S. Heywood to Oldham, January 4, 1922, Correspondence of J. H. Oldham, IMC Archives, London.
40. For a detailed analysis see:
    K. J. King 'The nationalism of Harry Thuku: a study in the beginnings of African politics in Kenya' in *Trans-African Journal of History*, Vol. I, No. I (39–53) on which the first two pages is based.
41. *Ibid.*, p.41.
42. *Ibid.*, p. 45.
43. Ross, 225.
44. King *op cit.*
45. Ross, p. 227.
46. Leakey to Mrs. Leakey, March 12, 1922, Mrs. Beecher's Private collections, Nairobi.
47. Native Resolutions of July 10, 1920 (Edinburgh House papers).
48. Leakey to Mrs. Leakey, March 12, 1922, Mrs. Beecher's Private Collections, Nairobi.
49. Hooper to Oldham, March 4, 1922, Correspondence of J. H. Oldham, IMC Archives, London.
50. For this see Chapter IV.
51. James Ngugi, *The River Between* (London, 1965), p. 74.

52. Arthur to Oldham, March 14, 1922, Correspondence of J. H. Oldham, IMC Archives, London.
53. Weithaga Bog Book, CMS, April 1922, p. 99, Bishop's Archives, Nairobi.
54. *Ibid.*
55. *Ibid.*
56. Leakey to Mrs. Leakey, March 16, 1922, Mrs. Beecher's Private Collections, Nairobi.
57. *Ibid.*
58. 'A Short History of the Kikuyu Province, 1911–1927,' p. 9, PC/CP/1/1/2 Nairobi Archives.
59. Chilver and Smith, History of East Africa, pp. 356–357.
60. Arthur to Oldham, November 17, 1922, Correspondence of J. H. Oldham, IMC Archives, London.
61. Hooper to Oldham, August 1, 1923 and March 14, 1923, Correspondence of J. H. Oldham, IMC Archives, London.
62. Leakey to Mrs. Leakey, March 12, 1922, Mrs. Beecher's Private Collections, Nairobi.
63. *Ibid.*
64. Harry Leakey to Mrs. Leakey, March 12, 1922, Mrs. Beechers Private Collections, Nairobi.
65. Oginga Odinga, *Net yet Uhuru* (London, 1967), pp. 27–28.
66. Carl Rosberg and John Nottingham, *The Myth of Mau Mau* (Praeger, 1966), p. 90.
67. Oginga Odinga, p. 29.
68. Johnstone Kenyetta to Lord Passfield, April 15, 1930, in the Correspondence between Kikuyu Central Association and the Colonial Office, 1920–1930.

7

The Parting of the Ways, 1875-1929

By 1914 the missionaries had established themselves on the highlands. They had gathered their adherents into mission stations, as they had done on the coast, in the nineteenth century, and this characterised their work during this period.

The missions established central stations in which they built central schools. From the central stations all the British protestant missions to Kenya established many out-schools. The CMS and the UFM established many of these on the Mombasa coast from the late seventies and by the end of the century many of them dotted the villages on the coast. The CMS repeated the same process on the highlands when it established itself there from the turn of the century. So too did the CSM, spreading out of its two strong central stations of Tumutumu and Kikuyu, which were also founded in the first decade of the century. By the twenties the highlands were dotted with out-schools.

The missionaries established schools because they believed that education was a vital weapon for evangelisation and they undertook the schooling of their converts because it was necessary for them to read the Bible and the catechism. Norman Leys characterised it thus:

When a mission begins work in a new district in Africa it begins with a school. . . . The primary object of the education given is to enable each person to learn for himself and to understand the record, the character and the teaching of Jesus and the chief doctrines of historical Christianity.[1]

But of greater importance was that the missionaries seriously believed that the evangelisation of Africa, and in this case the interior of Kenya, would inevitably be carried on by the Africans themselves. It was therefore necessary that those who passed through the central stations and schools should be literate in the Bible, since it was incumbent upon them to spread their influence and gospel among the rest. Writing as recently as 1956, but in effect reiterating Henry Venn's policy Roland Oliver said:

As Livingstone always foretold, the evangelisation of Africa could hardly begin until it was in the hands of native Africans as well as foreign missionaries. The fact that is so very little realised in Europe is that it is seldom indeed the white missionary who is in direct contact with the African pagan. In the beginning he was. He had to be. There was no one else. But almost his first task was to find and train the people who would ultimately succeed him; the twelve who, meanwhile, could man a dozen stations while he himself could occupy no more than one.[2]

Henry Parker, the second Bishop of East Equatorial Africa, in his memorandum to Salisbury Square, 1886, had emphasised this particular aspect of their work. He maintained that the fostering of the growth of a native agency was second only to the careful selection of Europeans. And this could only be brought about by having a 'careful educational system, probably including a Boarding school at Freretown, besides elementary schools at various stations, preparatory class for training of catechists and Native Pastors. . . .'[3] Bishop Parker was elaborating what already existed at Freretown for there was already a boarding school and a day school for both boys and girls. And at Ribe also the UFMC had a school.

Price included a central school in the plan put forward on the eve of the establishment of Freretown as a freed slave settlement. There was to be a central station to consist of 'a small congregation, a good elementary school, and by and by, one of a higher order together with a class of promising young men under special training as teachers and preachers, an industrial department and an Evangelistic Agency'.[4] At the Ribe UFMC mission station, Wakefield had, by the 1890s, established some form of school, mainly for adults, in Bible reading, while at the University's Mission in Zanzibar, established by Bishop Tozer in 1864, Frere found well-established schools in 1873.[5]

The CMS sent out its first headmaster, J. W. Handford, to start teaching the children of the freed slaves. He was also expected, as all missionaries were, to hold classes for adults to instruct them in the principles of Christianity.[6] By 1885 the CMS had made substantial progress in this direction. Taylor was able to report that he had found pupil teachers, trained by Handford, teaching ably in the schools. He said that there were classes for the people every day: 'Reading classes for the freed slaves, catechumens' classes, communicants and also teacher training.'[7] The following year, 1887, the CMS missionaries put forward a system whereby the Mission could retain the best boys who, they felt, were being lost from the mission. Henry Parker, therefore, put forward a plan whereby some boys would remain and be apprenticed but the best ones would pass on to be monitors and pupil teachers, readers, evangelists and pastors. Parker insisted that in the district schools at Chagga, Taita, Ugogo, Jilore, etc. it was necessary to teach the lower classes the vernacular of the place, and to teach the upper classes Swahili.[8] Those graduating from district schools would be admitted into the boarding school at Freretown. Here, the middle classes were instructed in Swahili, and Parker insisted that English should be taught as a foreign language in the two higher classes, the pupil teachers class and the one below.

The missionaries ran several classes in the central stations as work and enrolment increased, and, in time, they added Map Reading and Geography to the curriculum. All schools worked from an authorised syllabus drawn up by their executive committees. Each mission varied its scheme though they kept to the basic needs. Rev. T. S. England, reporting in the Diocesan Magazine in 1903, said, 'among the subjects taught are Reading, Writing, Arithmetic, Scripture, Map Drawing, Grammar, English and Needlework.'[9] In addition there was provision for the older boys to do agriculture in the afternoon, 'With the exception of three or four of whom we hope to make teachers,' noted Handford, 'older boys should do agriculture in the afternoon.'[10] Girls were also divided in classes. Their education was mainly in sewing and handicrafts, all aimed at preparing them for domestic work and motherhood.[11]

But the education of the young was not the only part of the

missionary propaganda. For more immediate purposes, and perhaps more important, the missions had to teach the adults and catechumens to read the Bible and some passages from the scriptures. The adult agents who, for various reasons, either connected with work on the mission or at their homes, could not attend school daily presented something of a problem. The missions, therefore, organised Sunday School classes for them or arranged evening classes on the evenings most convenient to them. Miss Harvey of CMS wrote:

In June I visited a class of women taught by Priscilla Bai, widow of George David. These are adults who come to us as freed slaves, different work it is to teach them, but I found they could nearly all repeat a different text and all those who did so received some coloured cotton and a needle.[12]

It was not necessary that these adults and catechumens should know how to write. Knowing the principles of Christianity for their immediate and even for their long term purposes meant ability to read simple translations of the Bible or selected passages of the Scriptures in the vernacular. Evangelists, too held village services for them. According to the *Kikuyu News*, these village services 'were the real fighting grounds in the battle against the awful mass of ignorance and superstition. . . .'[13]

All the missions therefore laid very strong emphasis on translating the Bible into vernaculars, in simple orthography, at the expense of academic linguistic perfection,[14] in order that the material could be made readily available to the adults in as simple a form as possible. It was important that they should be able to recite the passages and not that they should attain academic literary perfection. Growing clases made the necessity even greater. The CMS early realized the situation and so set up a subcommittee for translation work in 1887.[15] In 1910 the need to have a common form of orthography was even more necessary. Consequently, the Protestant Missions set up a subcommittee of the Alliance for translational work.[16] This became a very important subcommittee, and in the twentieth century, it eventually began to strive for academic perfection.

The CMS effort to turn out African evangelists and teachers since 1875 was crowned with the opening of a Divinity Class at

Freretown in 1888. In the eyes of the CMS at the time, this achievement was of supreme importance, for here would graduate all their future evangelists and teachers for all mission stations. William Price called July 6, 1888, the date the school was opened, a 'Red letter day' in the history of the CMS East Africa Mission. He said:

> We took the first steps in the formation of a training class for promising young men as Teachers and Evangelists. We began with a modest number of nine and (the) Rev. Fitch is the first Principal.[17]

All the best candidates from the district schools were admitted here to be trained as teachers and evangelists.

In 1904 the Buxton High School, named after the CMS Africa Secretary at Salisbury Square, and with a capacity to take between eight and 100 boarders, opened its doors to scholars.[18] It was, in fact, no more than a primary school although its name would seem to imply a higher standard, perhaps comparable to a modern high school. However, it fulfilled the function for which it was built. In his report of 1922, Jesse Jones said, 'in addition to the general instruction, it maintains a training course for teachers especially fitted to teach in districts where the language (Swahili) prevails'.[19] Religious instruction was compulsory and, in fact, comprised almost the whole of the curriculum at Buxton High School. It would, therefore, hardly have attracted any children from Muslim and Hindu families. However, it was the only school on the coast and, with the extra bribery the CMS seemed to have indulged in to attract scholars, they succeeded in enticing a few Mohammedans, exaggeratedly reporting that by 1910 these formed about 20% of the pupils.[20] The situation was seriously altered with the opening of a Roman Catholic School at Mombasa in 1908.[21] Government plans the same year for the opening of a secular school there further foreshadowed the near-collapse of the school, for none of the Muslims, Hindus and Pagans would in future be obliged to send their children to Buxton High School.[22] Before this date Buxton High School held the ground; Mr Martin the principal, reported:

> Numbers have trebled, standard of work has improved and the

teaching of the scriptures has borne good trust in many directions.[23]

The main drawback to the school, therefore, came to lie in its compulsory Christian nature, form and instruction in an area inhabited mainly by Muslim Swahili and Arabs, Hindus and Pagans. The CMS had early on realised its difficulties so they stepped up their campaign to gain converts by conducting instructions in Swahili, Gujerati, English and Arabic, but with very little success.[24] And the CSM were by 1911 claiming that they had apprentices to teacher training, medical work and technical industry in their central schools at Kikuyu and Tumutumu and they had run a girls' school since 1908.[25]

Among the boarders, the duration of stay at school and the content of their education varied from mission to mission. The demands placed upon the boarders at home and, surprisingly, in the missions, was far too great to insure continuous stay in the mission houses. For one thing, the boarding schools competed with parents for their children. Whether Kikuyu, Kamba, Nyika, or Chagga, there was always work assigned to the children, at different ages, in the family, and responsibility and work increased with age. The missions had, therefore, to contend with the more pressing needs demanded of the scholars in looking after goats and cattle, helping with farming and harvesting or, as in the case of girls, in education into the ways of adult life. This was, in fact, traditional education which Jomo Kenyatta says, 'begins with birth and ends with death'.[26] This would demand uninterrupted stay at home unless at a particular age education was to be done elsewhere. Hence the more reason for the parents' opposition to the mission house. In the tribal society where there was a very intricate educational system which involved training in matters of the family and the tribe, it was more meaningful and necessary for the children to stay at home regularly; their attendance at mission schools was a wasteful diversion from education of the young. The missionaries, however, thought otherwise.

This new system of education which involved living away from the family was not, according to the African, proper education. In the twenties, when opposition from parents was very violent, attendance, at best very irregular, at the various outschools was very small. In the boarding school regular schooling and classroom work was interrupted by the missionaries themselves, who used the boarders as servants and as labourers on the mission estates and surroundings. It is no exaggeration to say that the boarders did more physical work than classroom work. For example, the boarders at Taveta, of whom there were forty-two in 1895, had converted the mission settlement from a desert into what the *Taveta Chronicle* called a veritable garden.[27] That the *Taveta Chronicle* was able to call it 'Mahoo', meaning happy land, is ample testimony to the labour put into it by the boarders. And they had constructed a canal half a mile in length to irrigate the mission land.[28]

It was this very labour that the parents needed most. Over on the highlands, down in the Nyika plains or northwards along the coast and into the Tana River banks, the youth were needed to help with farming, and the girls to help with domestic tasks.

The difference between mission work and education and tribal work and education is clear and sharp. In the missions they were under the strict supervision of a white man; they learned to be Christians and, in time, to despise their home, family and tribe, while at home their daily family life trained them to be useful members of their society. In the missions they were required to cast out the old traditions, with the result that they became detribalised.

African parents, elders and headmen, therefore, opposed the establishment of schools and continued to do so, as they did the opening of a mission station, up to the beginning of the First World War. The CMS reported in 1909 that 'nearly all the schools in the interior (were) small for people failed to appreciate the advantages of education and many of them, in their hostility to Christianity refuse to allow their children to attend'.[29] Some even used force to keep their children at home. The CMS reported that their failure to open out-schools was due to the opposition of the headmen and chiefs.[30] Henry Scott reported to his mission that the boys attending the central school had been continuously persecuted. 'Again and again,' he wrote, 'we hear of a boy being beaten by his father because he will not desist from attending our village schools.'[31]

Most of the missions had to compromise or else face complete failure. The CSM had to declare a holiday for its school for the whole of April 1908, because most of the children remained at home to help with family work.[32] At Mombasa, at least in the early days, where the freed slaves were under the care of the CMS it was possible to ensure some form of regularity in school attendance by use of force. But with the adults it was not always possible to do so, since they had also to cultivate their plots of land for their own subsistence. 'The reading classes,' wrote J. W. Handford, 'have fallen off considerably and I do not press them at present for nearly every one is engaged in his shamba, either here or away at Maweni.'[33]

In the 1910s came reports from the Church of Scotland Mission that Nairobi had experienced similar effects on their schools. For example, it became increasingly difficult at Kikuyu, near Nairobi, to bring youths to school for training and to keep them there for a definite period of apprenticeship.

By 1916 out of a total of 32 schools in Kenya 31 were mission schools. Between then and 1921 the government built two more schools in addition to Machakos built in 1915: one at Waa and the other at Mwai both at Mombasa.[34] The Protectorate officials began to be perturbed by the sort of education that the missions were offering for it lacked the desired content. In 1918 one District Commissioner wrote:

The present form of education in missionary schools is not suitable for natives. A rudimentary knowledge of reading and writing is all that appears to be taught.[35]

It was clear that the missions had neither the funds nor the personnel for the task. So in 1917 J. Ainsworth, advisor for Native Affairs, proposed that the government and the missions should co-operate in the education of the Africans. His proposals formed a basis of discussion by the Education Commission formed in 1919 to advise on education in the Protectorate.[36] The commission on which J. W. Arthur represented the missions, recommended that the education of the Africans of Kenya should be left in the hands of the missions and the government should make grants in aid to the mission.[37] The government agreed to the recommendations but reserved the right of inspection. In 1920–1921 the government made block grants to the two major British protestant missions, the CMS and CSM.[38]

In 1923 the grants-in-aid rose to £4 305 out of the total expenditure on African education of £28 110. In the following year the expenditure on African education had risen by about £9 000, the total expenditure being £37 000.[39] Grants to missionary societies for the year 1924 were £10 346.[40]

It was not until the 1930s that the missions began to transform their educational system and began to provide for a four year primary school in their outstations and for teacher training colleges in the central stations. In the twenties the Africans showed a great demand for secular education, a demand which the missions were unable to meet notwithstanding government grants in aid. From 1920 on most of the missionaries working in Kenya began to report this demand to their home Committees. What is perhaps more interesting is that many of them readily admitted that they did not have the resources to meet this demand. In 1922 Harry Leakey of the CMS reported this overwhelming African desire for education, but at the same time sounded a word of caution as to what the Africans might do if the missions failed to meet their demand for non-religious education. He wrote:

> You cannot realise what it is like now, the Young Kikuyu are just crying for education, education, education, education. And if we can't give it them along with Christianity to satisfy their demands they mean to get it otherwise.[41]

It was certainly true that the mission could not give them this education most probably because of lack of funds and resources but also because they were primarily interested in providing for Christian education. Their early attempts to improve their schools in the 1920s failed. For example Kahuhia central school opened by the CMS in 1921 for the training of teachers faced closure in 1925 for lack of funds to run and maintain it. Elsewhere, as in the CMS schools at Mombasa and Kaloleni, the CMS was unable to fill in places which had been left vacant by the departure of its European staff.[42] Handley Hooper wrote:

> The CMS is too poor to undertake the training of teachers. We can continue with the expensive policy of maintaining European evangelists but the natives themselves will not agree

indefinitely nor would they be willing to assume financial responsibility indefinitely.[43]

The CMS faced the same problems at the same time. Horace Philp blamed his mission for its inability to cope with the ever-rising demand for African education even with government grants, saying: 'In fact it has been found necessary to temporarily suspend two important centres of activity and withdrawal from other outstations is under serious contemplation. Our financial position is our biggest embarrassment.'[44] Handley Hooper warned that the Africans would not rest content with this sort of situation. In a memorandum to the Bishop of Mombasa he pleaded with him to do the best he could to secure the assistance which the Home Committee 'evidently contemplates giving to missionary education in this country before its work has been hopelessly discredited by the defection of its pupils throughout a large area of its constituency'.[45] He further warned his committee of the widespread feeling among the African Christians that the CMS had failed to train enough Africans and they were in a state of near rebellion.[46]

By 1925 when the principle of grants in aid was in its fourth year, the new Principal of Jeanes School, J. W. C. Dougall, reported after tour of Mission Schools in Kikuyu that the CMS had not begun to take education seriously. Harry Thuku had demanded government schools rather than mission schools in 1921. African church elders openly told missionaries of their failure to give them the education that would enable them to get different kinds of employment. Representing this feeling was Peter Kigundu, a church elder, who told Hooper in 1924 that in all the twenty years that the CMS had been in Kikuyu it had not given the Africans the training and education which would fit them to carry out any responsibility.[47] Already the government was demanding higher standards in mission education as well as the reorganisation of its curricula as a condition for government grants. To meet this the missions indeed began some modest improvement: They withdrew from some of the outstations to concentrate on the central schools. However, the missions took the step at a wrong time when there was a demand for more and better schools. The Africans could only interpret this as a failure on the part of the mission as indeed it was.

The curriculum introduced by the missions was not liked by the Africans for it laid much emphasis on 'character training' rather than on academic standards. It further stressed manual training based on agriculture and technical training. The Representative Council of the Missions called for government aid for this undertaking, maintaining that 'all (were) agreed that the education of the Africans must be based on manual work'.[48] Technical education would in itself have been useful if it had not been all that the Africans were going to get in a country where such education could not qualify them for any other jobs except as manual workers and unskilled artisans. Indeed had they accepted such education it would have permanently placed them in an inferior position and it would have ensured that they remained second rate citizens as the settlers wanted them to.

This system was an adaptation of the Jeanes principle, first applied to Afro-American education in the southern parts of the United States, where Jeanes teachers, trained from the Jeanes Fund, had worked with success in Afro-American rural schools, particularly concentrating on the needs of the rural schools and communities.[49] The Phelps Stokes Commission recommended its application in Kenya.

In 1925 the Jeanes School was opened at Kabete in the highlands with funds obtained from the Carnegie Trust.[50] J. W. C. Dougall was its first Principal. The school concentrated on 'character training', and paid particular emphasis to practical subjects to meet the needs of Kenya African village communities. The different missions in Kenya selected teachers to spend two years in residence at the school. At Kabete the Jeanes teacher was taught new methods of teaching and new subjects relevant to the immediate needs of the community. On graduation, he went back to his community to impart this knowledge. *The Round Table* commented:

Without powers, without prestige, the Jeanes teacher goes back to his district to battle with custom, prejudice and disease, to teach and to inspire his people with enthusiasm for new things, and to do this without wasting or losing whatever may be of value in native life and custom as it now is to remake rural Africa.[51]

The Jeanes idea, permanently perpetuated, would have definitely placed the African in an inferior position in a world of science and technology that demanded higher education: It did this because it narrowed his needs and expectations to the confines of the community. However, it enjoyed popularity for a time although the opposition of the Africans made it impossible for it to become a permanent feature. The Jeanes era in Kenya African education ended in 1939. In 1927 fifteen Jeanes teachers graduated from Kabete; by 1931 there were thirty-six in the field.[52]

It over-emphasised that this was not what the Kikuyu wanted at all. From 1920 the Kikuyu wanted higher education to build a Kikuyu nation.[53] In 1925, some African parents requested government help to send their sons overseas for higher education.[54] Four years later, Jomo Kenyatta, Secretary of Kikuyu Central Association was asking for higher education for a Kikuyu nation.[55] The Advisory Committee on Native Education in Kenya, on which sat missionaries, settlers and government officials but with no Africans turned down this request.[56] They were to provide for it only as long as such education aimed at 'building up character', and as long as it was directed towards vocational training.[57] For the time being, no consideration was given to the request of the parents. So much emphasis on character training would seem to suggest that the African character was so bad that it required all the missionaries' life time to make it good. No mention was ever made of the character of the Europeans in Kenya, which needed more treatment than that of the African.

By 1925, the tide was moving too fast for either the missionaries or the settlers. That year local Native Councils were formed in Kenya.[58] Membership on these Councils was by election but the chairmen were to be the District Commissioners acting as ex-officio members.[59] The councils discussed matters directly concerning local affairs; they had no legislative power and this proved to be a very serious limitation. However, in some areas, they were given a free hand. They were given authority to levy local rates, to collect land fees and to raise a special levy for education.[60] All these they used, jealously and judiciously.

In their power to levy special rates for education, over and above that which was derived from direct taxation to the central government, lay the solution to their educational problem and a way out of the mission control of their education. Few then realised that they would use this power to collect money for secular schools which were to be out of the hands of the missions, and few even thought that their hopes would be realised four years hence. The frustration of the Africans with the mission education, and the mission control of this education was the main reason why they seized the opportunity offered them in the Native Councils to levy more money for their own education. In 1927 all the Councils in Kikuyu and Kavirondo voted money for education,[61] but only for government schools. This was two years before the female circumcision issue broke out. The Kikuyu Province Annual Report for 1929 reported that 'the Kikuyu demand for secular education and state as opposed to mission-controlled schools existed long before the circumcision question became acute'.[62] With regard to the educational levy and its purpose, the District Commissioner reported:

Ever since the Native Councils first voted money for education from their voluntary imposed rates, some three years ago they have asked for Government Schools and have declined to make over those sums for the enlargement and improvement of missions.[63]

In 1929, the Native Councils had in their local treasuries £50 000 ready cash for education.[64] The Director of Education said that this money was for the establishment of schools—'definitely for non-missionary schools.'[65] Between 1927 and 1929, the Native Councils of Fort Hall, Kiambu and Nyeri had collected £20 000 for this purpose.[66] District Commissioners all over Kikuyu had tried to use their official positions as chairmen of the councils to persuade the councils to make over this money to the missions, but had failed. It is no wonder that they began to be concerned. This feeling was well expressed by the District Commissioner of Fort Hall, who stated:

The Native Council has on deposit a sum of four thousand, seven hundred and fifty pounds for the erection of an un-demoninational Government School for the natives of the Reserve; this money has been on deposit for a considerable time, and both Councillors and natives are extremely disappointed that no start has been made with the building.[67]

Even the Director of Education tried to use his official capacity to force the councils to grant this money to the missions, but in vain. The Native Councils well knew that the policy of the government was that the government would only open government schools where no mission schools existed. But the councillors were already in rebellion. In a letter to Oldham, the Director of Education reported that the councils were bent on having none but government schools or else their own schools. He wrote:

First I discussed the matter with the Chief Native Commissioner and decided to go myself to the Local Native Councils. I wanted to know why they were asking for Government Schools when missionaries had been working so long among them. Then I asked the missionaries to address them. In the Kivirondo they want Government Schools. They have voted for Government Schools; in one case they said, tax was the money of all, irrespective of religion, and ought to be spent on all. In Kiambu, Arthur put the missionary case but he was completely turned down. The same consensus of opinion at Fort Hall.[68]

This put the government in a very difficult position. For one thing, this money was available at Kikuyu and Kavirondo, areas where the missions and their schools were most active and most firmly established.

Then the government could not argue that this was an uncalled for reaction against the missions by predominately pagan Councils. This was the view Arthur took, but one that was wrong, for, by 1929, three quarters of the Councillors in Kavirondo and Kikuyu were Christians.[69] Arthur also found it extremely difficult to believe that the councils' vote for government schools, or their own schools, which placed them definitely against mission schools was the general wish of all the natives of Kikuyu and Kavirondo. He consequently dismissed the councils as unrepresentative of the natives as a whole.[70] This was ridiculous since it came from a European who claimed to represent native interests in the Legislative Councils! Arthur's view about African political

F

associations was shared by the Colonial Government but it increasingly became more a convenient means of refusing to recognise them than the actual fact. Councillors to the Native Councils were elected through popular vote, and they discussed the very limited matters they were allowed to with the interests of the whole community at heart. Arthur blamed the District Commissioners for not directing the councils properly, by which he meant dictating to them what they should have done. It was soon clear that the government, even though under pressure from the missionaries, the CSM and the CMS in particular, could no longer continue to adhere to the principle agreed upon earlier that they would open schools only where there were no mission schools or places which could adequately be served by the missions. Even at Edinburgh House, Oldham believed that the pressure for native schools free from the hands of the missions was so great that it could not be contained; they wanted their own schools, from bush schools right to the top of the ladder.[71]

The demand for education contributed a great deal to the rise of Kikuyu nationalism which began with the formation of Kikuyu political associations in the early twenties. It is necessary to emphasise at once that this was not an inward-looking nationalism although the political associations were for the most part confined to the Kikuyu. They wanted education and in order to get the best kind of education it was necessary that they should themselves control and direct it. The failure of the missions to meet the increasing demand of the Kikuyu for education began to frustrate the Kikuyu from the beginning of the 1920s. Hence the ensuing struggle over the control of education. It is possible to see the struggle as a clash between two cultures: the missionaries stressed that theirs was superior and they sought to impart it to the Kikuyu through Christianity and western education. The Kikuyu on the other hand rejected such presumptions and emphasised that to remain Kikuyu they must continue to build a Kikuyu nation by building their own schools under their own control.

The opportunity for the final break with the missions which provided the Kikuyu with a *cause célèbre* to establish their own schools came over the circumcision issue. Perhaps there is nothing in the Kikuyu, the Chagga or the Gogo cultures (to mention only a few) which holds so central a place in the social life of the tribe or which strengthens the tribe's individual character as circumcision and the initiation ceremony which goes with this rite. Initially all girls and boys in the Kikuyu and other tribes were circumcised at puberty, thus graduating to womanhood or manhood.

By 1929, the opposition of the Kikuyu to the onslaught of the missions on the Kikuyu customs and traditions came to a head over the circumcision controversy. The Kikuyu Central Association, formed in 1925,[72] was in the vanguard of this movement. Arthur rightly said it stood for cultural identity.[73] However, he was wrong to equate KCA's stand for Kikuyu customs with anti-progressiveness and anti-order. But he believed it was so, because Kikuyuism clashed with the interests of the missions and what they stood for.

Almost all the Protestant missionaries to Kenya viewed all native customs and traditions with abhorrence. They saw nothing good in African dances, music or in such important African traditions as circumcision and initiation ceremonies. They lumped them together as heathen and immoral without trying to understand them, what they were for and what significance they had in the life of the people to whom they had come to teach Christianity. No African, according to the Missionaries, could become Christian before giving up his old, treasured customs. Invariably they used moral reasons for political ends. During the Harry Thuku movement Arthur persuaded the government to ban the anti-European and anti-missionary songs and dances of the Kikuyu by maintaining that 'they were morally bad and the words and bodily action incites to passion and results invariably in *umbani* (fornication)'.[74]

For the Kikuyu circumcision marked the end of one life and the beginning of another. After circumcision, the person was henceforth accepted into the society as an adult man or woman, ready and able to discharge responsibility required of all Kikuyu women and men.

The CSM was opposed to female circumcision from the very beginning of their work on the highlands. In 1909, the CSM came out in the open against initiation ceremonies and ruled that boys could be circumcised but without the rites connected with it.[75] In 1925, the CSM missionaries had brought enough pressure to bear on their staff at Kikuyu to make them agree, against their will, that no Christians should practise circumcision.[76] In the following year, again under pressure from Arthur and his staff, the African Church Committee recommended 'total prohibition'.[77] That year the CSM made non-circumcision for girls a necessary condition for church membership and further ruled that those who condoned it were liable to excommunication. By the first year of the second decade, the Church of Scotland Mission had ruled against circumcision in all its Christians, and the Gospel Missionary Society and the American Inland Mission had also joined them.[78] Arthur campaigned to get the government to legislate against it, and persuaded the Roman Catholics to join a deputation of the Kenya Missionary Alliance to see the governor, on July 5, 1926, on the subject of the suppression of indecent customs.[79] However, the view of the government, which was also the view of the CMS, was that circumcision held such a central place in the life of the Kikuyu, and it was of so ancient an origin, that it could not be abolished by legislation only through education.[80] In a confidential circular from the Native Affairs Department, the acting Chief Native Commissioner, C. F. Watkins, admitted in 1925 that, in its more restricted form, female circumcision did no harm.[81] He stated that legislation to prevent it would be difficult to enforce and that premature action would only unite the natives against the government in defence of their old customs.[82] Watkins preferred to bring it to an end through education when Kikuyu public opinion would be well-educated enough to stop female circumcision of its own free will.

The CMS did not adopt a uniform policy towards circumcision.[83] At Kahuhia, Handley Hopper conducted regular lessons against circumcision; at Kabete, the CMS steered the same course as the CSM, and in the rest of the stations the missionaries did nothing.[84] In 1927 the Highland Missionary Committee of the CMS had resolved to support every effort put forward to discourage female circumcision.[85] The committee did this after the District Council of the African Church Council had requested that 'means be found for the training apart of those girls who wish not to be circumcised'.[86] But the bishop outlined the policy of the CMS on the issue only in 1931. In his pastoral letter the bishop set out the conditions on which the CMS would tolerate female circumcision until such time as the African Christians of the CMS became sufficiently educated to secure its abolition. The bishop laid down three conditions:[87]

1 All heathen practices connected with the custom must be entirely abandoned by Christians.
2 Anything of a public nature must be strictly prohibited.
3 Any operation causing physical injury to the individual must be forbidden.

The Methodist Church refused to accept that an African could not be a member of Christ 'according to his lights, and cannot be a member of His Church, while continuing to practise or condone a custom based upon long tribal tradition'.[88] R. T. Worthington, writing on behalf of the MMS, further seriously questioned the right of Europeans to lay down the condition on which an African may be regarded as a member of the Church of Christ. He wrote:

The function of the Church is not to impose upon any community a set of regulations but to introduce men and women of every race to the perfect life, helping them as it may mean for them, but realising that only from within can come growth in Christlikeness, and recognition that no set pattern of Christlikeness can be imposed on Africans and Europeans alike.[89]

There is little doubt, now, that the reports of the missions stating that the African church leaders agreed that laws should be passed against female circumcision, is not correct. The same applied to the reports that the Native Councils, under pressure from the District Commissioners, did so. None of them took it seriously, and they did not enforce the rules they had passed. It was not uncommon for the missionaries to use force to get their adherents to do what they wanted them to do. African opposition to the rule that Christian girls should not be circumcised was sporadic before the second half of the decade. Matters came to a head in 1928 when at a political rally held at Nyeri that year, the Kikuyu Central Association declared that they stood for Kikuyu nationalism and stated openly that they wanted female circumcision.[90] The African Church leaders at Tumutumu who were members of the Kikuyu Central Association declared that they would repudiate the law at Tumu-Tumu introduced in 1926, when the church was attacked and their school destroyed.[91] When the CSM required a declaration of loyalty from the church members, the Church met with a rebellion and lost over 200 members.

Events became more dramatic as the CSM and the Kikuyu Central Association prepared for Armageddon. The following year, a conference of the representatives of the missions passed resolutions against female circumcision. The KCA used the resolutions in their political platform to make known the intention of the missions to erode Kikuyu culture. Legal suits taken at Kiambu, where two women were fined thirty shillings for performing a severe operation, only enhanced the popularity of the Kikuyu Central Association.[92]

The CSM took the lead in requiring the African leaders of the church to sign an oath, as a prerequisite for continued membership in the church.[93] Mr A. Irvine, from Chogoria CSM mission, said that he and Arthur felt that it was right to demand from their church members absolute separation from political activity which was so definitely anti-Church and anti-Christian.[94] J. W. Arthur pressed the Kirk Session to agree that African Church leaders of the CSM should swear an oath 'requiring them to reaffirm their vow against this rite, and to dissociate themselves from the particular political party (Kikuyu Central Association) which was responsible for the agitation'.[95] The presbytery approved the wish of the Kirk Session, though by no means unanimously; Arthur reported that there was a dissenting minority in the presbytery.[96] The oath demanded:

I promise to have done with everything connected with circumcision of women because it is not in agreement with the things of God, and to have done with the Kikuyu Central Association because it aims at destroying the Church of God.[97]

At Chogoria, the CSM faced great opposition to the oath, and only fourteen members signed the oath along with two children.[98] This evidently shows that only a few of the very staunchest remained true to the Church of Christ.[99] Attendance at the CSM Central School fell by half, while, out of a regular attendance of

1 529 in four out-schools, there were only 48 pupils.[100] The effect it had on their teachers was even more startling; in November, 1929, Dougall reported that some twenty to thirty out-school teachers had left, and that only three were left in the Central Station.[101] Stevenson Githii, an African Christian of CSM had this to say about the results:

> we do not get many worshippers in our services.... We also get very few people in the Central School, Kikuyu and none in our out-stations. In the evening of Christmas Day, Dr Arthur, Barlow, Gilbert, Andrea, Samuel, Gitau ... and myself had to walk in darkness to see and arrest the turned back Mission boys who were dancing a bad new dance in the Mission after the Government had prohibited dancing that bad dance in the Mission land and Reserves.[102]

Before the end of 1929, the Kikuyu had boycotted all the out-schools of the CSM, AIM and GMS. The prestige of these missions suffered considerably, while the influence and activities of the KCA increased greatly as a result of this conflict. For example, the KCA political hostility against the CSM station, Chogoria, in Embu district, received unprecedented support from the masses in the last four months of 1929.[103] The KCA was so successful in mustering all the forces against the CSM on this issue that the District Commissioner reported that nothing else could have raised the prestige of the association so high as did the *ruling of the mission against circumcision.*[104] The CMS at Fort Hall and Embu, however, was comparatively little affected and the United Methodist Mission was not affected at all for they had adopted a very compromising policy towards this issue.[105]

The political ferment was now openly violent and anti-missionary. Remote mission out-stations had suffered scattered attacks, schools and church services had been interrupted and stopped, and coffee seedlings pulled out of the mission gardens since 1926.[106] Tumutumu CSM station is a spectacular example.[107]

Throughout 1929 open attack on the missions became widespread across Kikuyu. In essence, violence became now a popular way through which the Kikuyu, and here Kikuyu becomes synonimous with the Kikuyu Central Association, expressed their hostility against the missions. At Gacharage, Kiambu district, an armed group of thirty young Kikuyu pulled down the roof of the school building.[107] They would have completely destroyed it had not the Rev. Mr Bewes arrived in time to save it from destruction and the teacher from being beaten.[108] At Ngeca, also Kiambu district, Welbourn reported the same thing; the evangelist was ordered to stop conducting church services, school apparatus and furniture were removed and gardens destroyed.[109] Towards the last two years of the decade, the Kikuyu had begun to launch claims to the land on which the missions had built, but in vain. In 1929, the District Commissioner at Kiambu, reported that the natives were claiming the estate, which then belonged to the White Sisters there, and the land of the Scotch Mission, Kikuyu, and of the Africa Inland Mission, at Kijabe.[110] Their resolve to use force to recover the land which they had freely given the missions is understandable, the more so since the Africans had, in addition to giving the land, built the schools and the church buildings with their own labour and money, a process which was therefore, no mean investment. These were, after all, the schools which had made the government refuse to open government schools for the Kikuyu. In a real sense everything in the missions belonged to the Africans, and it is not surprising that after failing to get them back legally, the Africans resorted to force. The climax was reached on January 2, 1930, with the murder of Hilda Stumpf of Kijabe, AIM station.[111] Catechists and school-masters who were in control of the out-schools became subject to direct presonal attack and abuse for they were seen as stooges and collaborators of the missionaries. Their refusal to take a stand with the majority of the Christians who had stood for Kikuyu cultural nationalism and had repudiated the church law against female circumcision, placed them in the same position as those who refused to support the Mau Mau twenty years later. Fortu-ately for them they were not killed as their counterparts came to be but they suffered equal abuse and direct personal attack.

By 1930, the break with the missions was already under way. In Kiambu, Fort Hall and Embu, numerous requests were made to the government officials for permission to hold independent religious meetings. New sects had already appeared by the beginning of the year. In Kiambu, for example, five independent churches were established.[112] According to the Provincial Report for 1930, they were well attended and were conducted on more or less normal lines.[113] Arthur sadly reported that those who had left his church had begun to hold opposition services; not in the spirit of Christ, he mistakenly said, but in a spirit of rebellion.[114] This was contrary to the more accurate and sober reports of the District Commissioners of the various districts.

The Kikuyu Christians had now come into their own, and were ready to begin and lead their own churches. These churches were to be independent—that independence from European church control that they had been trying to get since 1922.

In the educational field, there had been a deadlock since 1927. There was no government school in Kikuyu country primarily because the policy of the government was to open schools only where there were no mission schools. The deadlock occurred because the Native Councils were unwilling to hand over to the missions the considerable sums they had voted for education, and the government strictly adhered to the policy of 'establishing schools only on the ground of the absence or inadequacy of missionary effort'.[115] J. Scott put the blame for this anti-missionary attitude in the councils on Arthur. He maintained 'he (Arthur) has gone out on the rails and has apparently captivated Downing of the AIM'.[116] He further accused him of chastising his teachers which he said was persecution.[117]

Scott was backed by a good number of missionaries. Handley Hooper, now Africa Secretary at Salisbury Square, took a more sympathetic view of the situation,[118] feeling that the natives had come to realise that in the last analysis they could not force the missions to give them the education they wanted since the Africans felt the responsibility lay directly with the giver. On the other hand, government services in education, as in all other services, were rendered in respect of revenue directly collected from them. It was therefore necessary to control it; and this was why they wished so persistently to have a direct say in the control of their destiny which education would help shape. Hooper, however, lamented the wide gap between the Africans and the missions as the demand for Africans to control their own education reflected nothing else but, he believed, 'a woeful lack of confidence between the missions and the natives'.[119] Of Arthur, he wrote:

Except for a small group around Kikuyu, the majority of

F*

natives have no confidence in him (Arthur). He is essentially the old Tory of the ruling caste and does not get down amongst them enough to make them feel he is one of them. Some of his staff at Kikuyu call him Lord Arthur. There is a trace of truth in it, for he is essentially a clean sports loving Sahib.[120]

Towards the end of 1929 African parents petitioned the Director of Education to open schools for their children. In January, 1930, Zakaria Wambura, Barnaba Reguru and Zefania Wainaina saw the Director as representatives of the parents who wanted the government to open schools between Dagoretti and Kikuyu, where the CSM had had schools.[121] The Director of Education had done his best to keep up the already sinking reputation of the church by refusing to open government schools in Kikuyu. However, while he was pleading for the churches to come to peaceful terms with their adherents, the Africans were already establishing independent native schools, much against his wish. In 1930, all the District Commissioners in Kikuyu had become doubtful as to the wisdom and the advantages of giving a monopoly of all African education to the missions.[122] They were all agreed that it would be impossible to maintain the system which was primarily for the Africans who were bitterly opposed to this monopoly. There was no other course open to the government except to co-operate fully with the Native Councils so as to maintain control and supervision over the new schools. The Provincial Commissoiner, in his Annual Report, Kikuyu Province emphasised the importance and the urgency of the question of education. He pointed out that it was necessary for the government to be positive towards the demands of the Kikuyu for education, lest the government lose the confidence of the natives and hence the control of African education.[123] He called for the government to take the opportunity offered in the movement, and establish control over the educational organisation before the movement gathered too much momentum to be controlled effectively.[124]

It was already too late. By 1929 the Kikuyu established independent churches and schools. African churches and schools were part of the same movement and one is inseparable from the other. As proof of the fact that these schools were meant to be authentically Kikuyu and to foster Kikuyu cultural nationalism the Kikuyu Karing'a Education Association was formed by which Karing'a meant authentic Kikuyu culture.[125] In 1930 the Githunguri Teachers' College was formed for higher education and for the training of the teachers for the Kikuyu independent schools.[126]

The development of the independent schools and churches after 1930 lies outside the scope of this study. The movement for this African independence was hard and long having begun in 1922. It must be remembered that from 1930 there existed side by side mission and government schools and western churches on the one hand and African independent schools and churches on the other hand. The former became training centres for those who would serve the colonial administration and from which graduated some of the so called 'Loyalists' of the emergency era while the latter produced Kikuyu who waged the war to regain the independence of Kenya.

Whatever one might say about the shortcomings of the independent schools and churches, and there have been many who have criticised them from the conventional western viewpoint, few will deny that by 1930 a substantial number of the Africans in Kikuyuland had succeeded in cutting themselves loose from the mission-controlled schools with their colonial orientation by establishing their own schools whose curricula, administration and destiny lay entirely in their own hands. What is more, they now had some control of education, a powerful ideological weapon which the missions and the colonial administration had used with some success to domesticate the Africans and to make them subservient to the colonial masters.

There is little doubt that these schools and the Githunguri Teachers College served as ideological centres for the training of Mau Mau fighters. Many of their graduates were taught to reject the patronage of the missions and the colonial administration; in short to reject alien rule and to become true to the Kikuyu nation that is. Kikuyu *karing'a*. This ideology was essential for the ensuing armed nationalist struggle of the late forties and fifties.

Due credit must therefore be accorded to the leaders of the Kikuyu Central Association and the Kenya African Union under the valiant leadership of Mzee Jomo Kenyatta who led the struggle for and succeeded in establishing their own schools independent of those of the government and of the missions. The harsh realities of the settler-dominated colony which was backed by an increasingly suppressive colonial administration almost strangled the African independent schools in the thirties. Certainly in 1940 the administration imposed a ban on the KCA. Nevertheless the graduates of the independent schools remained to wage the Mau Mau war of 1952–1956 which led to the liquidation of British rule in Kenya. These bear full testimony to the success of the independent schools in inculcating the right kind of nationalist ideology into the minds of those who passed through them. Independence in Kenya was won through the armed struggle which they waged in the forests under very difficult conditions. One hopes that true *Uhuru*, which some maintain has not yet come to a majority of those who fought in the forest, will soon come and so testify even more fully to the contribution made by the independent schools to the regaining of the independence of Kenya in 1963.

NOTES

1. Norman Leys, *Kenya* 2nd ed., 1925, p. 212.
2. Roland Oliver, *How Christian is Africa?* (London, 1956), p. 9.
3. Henry Parker, 'Memorandum to the CMS,' September 5, 1886, G3 A5/03, CMS Archives, London.
4. William Salt Price to Hutchinson, June 19, 1873, C A5/017, CMS Archives, London.
5. Bartle Frere to Lang, January 5, 1886, G3 A5/03, CMS Archives, London.
6. J. Handford to Lang, January 5, 1886, G3 A5/03, CMS Archives, London.
7. W. Taylor to Lang, January 5, 1886, G3 A5/03, CMS Archives, London.
8. Parker to Lang, January 18, 1887, G3 A5/04, CMS Archives, London.
9. T. S. England, Report in the *Diocesan Magazine*, CMS, October, 1903, p. 3.
10. Handford to Fenn, July 25, 1876, G3 A5/011, CMS Archives, London, D. A. Hooper to Baylis, December 16, 1910, G3 A5/018, CMS Archives, London.
11. E. Fitch to Lang, May 24, 1889, G3 A5/06, CMS Archives, London.
12. *Extracts, Annual Letters*, CMS, 1887, pp. 344–345.
13. *Kikuyu News*, August 4, 1908, pp. 3–4.
14. J. F. Ade Ajayi, *Christian Missions in Nigeria 1841–1891: The Making of a New Elite* (London, 1965), p. 131.

15. Shaw to Lang, June 30, 1887, G3 A5/04, CMS Archives, London.
16. Henry Scott to Maclachlan, September 24, 1908, MS 7607, National Library of Scotland Archives.
17. Price to Lang, August 29, 1888, G3 A5/05, CMS Archives, London.
18. Martin to Baylis, January 28, 1910, G3 A5/018, CMS, London.
19. Jesse Jones, *Education in East Africa* (New York, 1924), p. 115.
20. Martin to Baylis, January 28, 1910, G3 A5/018, CMS, London.
21. *Ibid.*
22. *Ibid.*
23. *Ibid.*
24. *CMS Proceedings*, 1905–1906, p. 56.
25. J. W. Arthur, 'Church of Scotland Mission in Kikuyu,' unpublished typed manuscript, Arthur Papers, University of Edinburgh Archives.
26. Jomo Kenyatta, *Facing Mount Kenya* (London, 1938), p. 99.
27. *Taveta Chronicle*, I, 1895, pp. 3–4.
28. *CMS Proceedings*, 1894–1895, pp. 84–85.
29. *Ibid.*, 1908–1909, pp. 51–54.
30. *Kikuyu News*, June 11, 1911, p. 2.
31. *Ibid.*, April 23, 1909, p. 6.
32. *Ibid.*, April 6, 1908, p. 5.
33. Handford to Lang, February 5, 1885, G3 A5/04, CMS Archives, London.
34. Jones, Jesse, *Education in East Africa*, p. 119.
35. District Commissioner to Provincial Commissioner Mombasa, November 7, 1918. Coast 16/38, Kenya National Archives, Nairobi.
36. Arthur to Father, November 19, 1919, Arthur Papers, University of Edinburgh Archives.
37. Arthur to Oldham, May 14, 1921, Correspondence of J. H. Oldham, IMC Archives, London.
38. Hooper to Oldham, June 20, 1927, Correspondence of J. H. Oldham, IMC Archives, London.
39. Jones, p. 111.
40. *Ibid.*
41. Harry Leakey to Mrs Leakey, October 26, 1922, Personal letters of Harry Leakey, 1900–1923, in the private collections of Mrs J. I. Beecher, Nairobi (cited hereafter as Mrs Beecher's Private Collections).
42. Hooper to Oldham, June 30, 1925, Correspondence of J. H. Oldham, IMC Archives, London.
43. *Ibid.*
44. *Kikuyu News*, June 25, 1927, pp. 15–16.
45. Hooper to Oldham, December 1, 1924, enclosing Memorandum to Bishop of Mombasa, Correspondence of J. H. Oldham, IMC Archives, London.
46. Hooper to G. T. Manley, June 30, 1925, Correspondence of J. H. Oldham, IMC Archives, London.
47. Hooper to Oldham, December 5, 1924, Correspondence of J. H. Oldham, IMC Archives, London.

48. Minutes of the Representative Council of the Protestant Alliance, Kenya, November 19–22, 1923, Correspondence of J. H. Oldham, IMC Archives, London.

49. For a study of the Jeanes Schools and the application of the Jeanes ideas in the southern parts of the United States, see Lance Jones, *The Jeanes Teachers in the United States* (New York, 1937).

50. 'An Experiment in African Education in Kenya.' In the *Round Table*, xx, June 1930, p. 565.

51. *Ibid.*, p. 565.

52. Groves, G. P. *The Planting of Christianity in Africa*, IV, (2nd ed. 1958), p. 117.

53. Jomo Kenyatta to Editor, *Muingwithania*, April, 1929, translated into English by the CID, AC/MKS IB/13/1 Kenya National Archives, Nairobi (cited hereafter as Nairobi Archives).

54. Director of Education to the Senior Commissioner, October 17, 1925, enclosing Minutes and Resolutions of the Advisory Committee on Native Education, Kenya, Coast 31/431, Nairobi Archives.

55. Jomo Kenyatta to Editor, *Muigwithania*, April, 1929, AC/MKS B/13/1, Nairobi Archives.

56. Director of Education to the Senior Commissioner, October 17, 1925, enclosing Minutes and Resolutions of the Advisory Committee on Native Education, Kenya, Coast 31/431, Nairobi Archives.

57. *Ibid.*

58. Vincent Harlow, E. M. Chilver and Alison Smith, *History of East Africa*, Vol. II (Oxford, 1965), p. 350.

59. *Ibid.*

60. *Ibid.*

61. Provincial Annual Reports, Kikuyu Province, 1929, PC/CP. 15/2/1, Nairobi Archives.

62. *Ibid.*

63. *Ibid.*

64. John Scott to Oldham, March 10, 1929, Correspondence of J. H. Oldham, IMC Archives, London.

65. *Ibid.*

66. Provincial Annual Reports, Kikuyu Province, 1930, PC/CP.15/2/1, Nairobi Archives.

67. *Ibid.*

68. Scott to Oldham, March 10, 1929, Correspondence of J. H. Oldham, IMC Archives, London.

69. Scott to Oldham, June 7, 1929, Correspondence of J. H. Oldham, IMC Archives, London.

70. Scott to Oldham, January 5, 1929, Correspondence of J. H. Oldham, IMC Archives, London.

71. Oldham to Hooper, March 11, 1930, Correspondence of J. H. Oldham, IMC Archives, London.

72. Harlow, Chilver and Smith, *History of East Africa*, p. 358.

73. Arthur to Mclachlan, March 9, 1929, in J. W. Arthur Papers, Univer-

sity of Edinburgh Library Archives, Edinburgh. (Cited hereafter as Arthur Papers, University of Edinburgh Archives.)

74. Arthur to Chief Native Commissioner, November 17, 1922, Arthur Papers, University of Edinburgh Archives.

75. F. B. Welbourn, *East African Rebels, A Study of Some Independent Churches* (London, 1961), p. 136.

76. *Ibid.*

77. *Ibid.*

78. *Ibid.*

79 Minutes of the Kenya Missionary Council, August 17, 1926, Correspondence of J. H. Oldham, IMC Archives, London.

80. Native Affairs Department Circular No. 36, 'Female Circumcision', September 21, 1925 (Confidential), KBU/32 Nairobi Archives.

81. *Ibid.*

82. *Ibid.*

83. Church of Scotland, 'Memorandum on Circumcision,' December 1, 1931 (unpublished manuscript), p. 9, Arthur Papers, University of Edinburgh Archives.

84. *Ibid.*, 13–15.

85. Minutes of the Highlands Missionary Committee, CMS, October 25–26, 1927, Bishop's Archives, Nairobi.

86. Minutes of the Highlands Missionary Committee, CMS, January 6, 1927, Bishop's Archives, Nairobi.

87. Bishop Heywood to All Clergy and Members of the Pastorate Committee in the Diocese, October 12, 1931 in file marked 'Circumcision,' Bishop's Archives, CMS, Nairobi.

88. Notes on the attitude of the Methodist Missionary Society in Connection with the 'Circumcision of Girls,' by R. T. Worthington, n.d., in file marked 'Circumcision.' Bishop's Archives, CMS, Nairobi.

89. *Ibid.*

90. Arthur to Oldham, September 2, 1930, Correspondence of J. H. Oldham, IMC Archives, London.

91. *Ibid.*

92. Dagoretti Political Record Book IV, p. 55. KBU/8Q. Nairobi Archives.

93. *Kikuyu News*, June 20, 1930, pp. 4–5.

94. A. Irvine to Editor, *Kikuyu News*, September 28, 1929.

95. *Kikuyu News*, June 20, 1930, p. 5.

96. *Ibid.*

97. A. Irvine to Editor, *Kikuyu News*, September 28, 1929.

98. *Ibid.*

99. *Ibid.*

100. Arthur to Duchess of Atholl, January 17, 1930, Correspondence of J. H. Oldham, IMC Archives, CMS, London.

101. Dougall to Oldham, November 10, 1929, Correspondence of J. H. Oldham, IMC Archives, London.

102. 'An African View of the Crisis,' in *Kikuyu News*, December 29, 1930, p. 3.

103. Kikuyu Province, Annual Report, 1929, CP/PC 15/2/1, Nairobi Archives.
104. *Ibid.*
105. *Ibid.*
106. District Commissioner, Kiambu, to Provincial Commissioner, Nyeri, December 19, 1929, PC/DC Adm. 15/3/3, Nairobi Archives.
107. *Ibid.*
108. *Ibid.*
109. Welbourne, p. 141.
110. District Commissioner, Kiambu, to Provincial Commissioner, Nyeri, December 24, 1929, PC/DC Adm. 15/3/3.
111. *Ibid.*
112. Kikuyu Province, Annual Report, 1930, PC/CP 15/2/1, Nairobi Archives.
113. *Ibid.*
114. *Kikuyu News*, June 20, 1930, p. 5.
115. Kikuyu Province, Annual Report, 1930, PC/CP 15/2/1, Nairboi Archives.
116. Scott to Oldham, December 14, 1929, Correspondence of J. H. Oldham, IMC Archives, London.
117. *Ibid.*
118. Hooper to Oldham, April 11, 1929, Correspondence of J. H. Oldham, IMC Archives, London.
119. *Ibid.*
120. *Ibid.*
121. Scott to Oldham, January 9, 1930. Correspondence of J. H. Oldham, IMC Archives, London.
122. Kikuyu Province, Annual Report, 1930, PC/CP 15/2/1, Nairobi Archives.
123. *Ibid.*
124. *Ibid.*
125. I am greatly indebted to Grant Kamenju, Department of Literature, University of Dar es Salaam for the meaning and explanation of this and many other Kikuyu sayings and aphorisms.
126. *Ibid.*

Bibliography

PRIMARY SOURCES

I *Archival Material*

1 *Missionary Sources in Kenya*
The Archbishop of East Africa Archives, Nairobi, Kenya. Now at the University of Nairobi, Kenya.

a Files marked: (Correspondence with) Chief Native Commissioner 1918–1939.
CMS Correspondence 1929–1959.
Diocese of Mombassa—Cumulative Minutes.
Minute Books (five in number).
Province of East Africa—in process of formation 1927–1960, Vols. I–IV.
Highland Missionary Committee—Correspondence 1931–1952, Minutes (typed) 1922–1940.
Circumcision.
Alliance School 1926–1940.

b Packets marked: Letters to 1913.
Diocesan Records 1880, 1911, Bishop Peel, etc.

c Diary of Mary Bassett 1892–1895 (in personal keeping of Mrs J. L. Beecher, Nairobi). (Mary Bassett married Harry Leakey in 1899 and Mrs J. L. Beecher is their daughter.)

d Personal letters of Canon H. Leakey 1909–1923, also in the personal keeping of Mrs Beecher.

e The Archbishop's library has invaluable source materials which are not classified.

The Bishop of Mombasa Archives, Mombasa, Kenya
Almost all the documents have been transferred to London, Salisbury Square or to the Archives of the Archbishop, Nairobi. Some unclassified material remains.
Regional Secretary of East Africa (CMS) Nairobi
Unclassified material exists here. Of particular interest are the Minute Books and Log Books of CMS Mission Stations, Mombasa Diocese. These have been transferred to the Archives of the Archbishop, Nairobi, and now to the University of Nairobi.
Church of Scotland Mission Kikuyu Archives
All have been transferred to Edinburgh University Archives or the National Library of Scotland.

2 *Missionary Sources in the United Kingdom*

Church Missionary Society Archives, Salisbury Square (CMS), *East Equatorial Africa Mission:*
    Incoming papers from the East Equatorial Mission, 1844–1873, classified under C A5/MI-, 1874–1915 classified under G3 A5/O.
    Outgoing letters from the Secretary, Salisbury Square to East Equatorial Africa Mission classified under C A5/LI (1842–1877), C A5/L2, (1877–1883); G3 A5/L3 (1883–1886), G3 A5/L4 (1886–1888); G3 A5/L5 (1888–1890), G3 A5/L6 (1890–1893), G3 A5/L7 (1893–1896), G3 A5/L8 (1896–1901), G3 A5/L9 (1901–1906), G3 A5/LIO (1906–1916).
Church of Scotland Mission, Kikuyu Archives at

a *National Library of Scotland*, transferred thither after the war from the Archives of the Foreign Missions Committee of the Church of Scotland. (A fair number of the records are missing.)
Correspondence in record books:
East Africa Scottish Mission 1891–1898 classified as: MS 8015–16.
Convenor of the Foreign Missions Committee, MS 7534–40.
Secretary of the Foreign Missions Committee, MS 7541–54, MS 7556–7605.
Letters to Secretary of Foreign Missions Committee, MS 7606–17: (a) Letters from Missionaries (East and Central Africa) MS 7606–8; (b) General Letters MS 7612–17, MS 7625.

b *The University of Edinburgh Library Archives:*
J. S. Arthur Papers in packets marked: Kikuyu Land Question 1901–1937; Native Labour Question, 1901–1925; Kikuyu Missions Volunteer Corps, 1917–1918; Miscellaneous Subjects, 1901–1933; Missions general.

G. A. Grieve Papers—two files mainly on Alliance High School of which he became the first principal in 1926.

c *International Missionary Council Archives* (Correspondence of J. H. D. Oldham)
Documents are preserved in packets marked: Africa—General; East Africa—Kenya relevant files marked 'Currency changes', 'Native Unrest', 'Political Situation', 'Land', 'Native Labour', 'Indians—Protest (1921–23)', 'Education', 'Correspondence (J. W. Arthur, H. D. Hooper, etc., 1920–1930)'.

d *The Methodist Missionary Society, Marylebone Road* (United Methodist Free Church)
Only three minute books of the Foreign Missionary Committee have survived. All attempts to trace both outgoing letters to the Kenya Mission and the incoming letters from the Kenya Mission at the time of my visit to England or before have produced no results.
The three large minute books are classified under: Foreign Missionary Committee Minute Book I (1862–1907); Unnumbered Minute Book (1908–1923); Minute Book II (1824–1940).

3 *Government Sources in Kenya*

a *National Archives, Jogoo House, Nairobi*
All the Kenya Government records are now held at the Central Archives in Nairobi in the basement of Jogoo House. By early 1965 almost all the records from all the provincial and district headquarters of Kenya were at Nairobi. By 1966 most of the records were already classified and the Archives were open for research. The records to 1945 are open but the Archivist with the approval of the Permanent Secretary, Office of the Vice President, can grant special permission for use of documents through 1960. Except for the Secretariat records for the East African Protectorate Administration which were destroyed by fire in 1939, the Archives are very complete and they are the main source of historical research in Kenya.

b *Provincial Archives, Mombasa*
The author was at Mombasa from May through June, 1966 and part of September, 1966. Most of the records had been transferred to Nairobi and those still at Mombasa were in the process of being transfered to Nairobi. The Provincial Archives, however, hold a few useful records which are open to researchers upon permission from the headquarters at Nairobi. Before the end of 1966 these records were open to members of the Univer-

sity of East Africa without prior permission from Nairobi but the Kenya government has now adopted strong regulations for the use of government documents.

4 *Government Sources in the United Kingdom, Public Records Office, London*

a *Foreign Office Records*
Series F.O.84, Slave Trade. Correspondence relating to East Africa, volumes marked 'Zanzibar', and 'Domestic Various'. F.O.403, Africa—Confidential Prints. F.O.2, Africa (General), Zanzibar Correspondence 1898–1905. F.O.107, 'Zanzibar'—Correspondence relating to East Africa 1893–1898.

b *Colonial Office Records*
Series C.O.533. Correspondence relating to East Africa Protectorate/Kenya from 1905.

II *Interviews*

Most of the interviews were taken at random as and when the occasion arose during my research about Kikuyu and Mombasa. Recorded interviews were, however, conducted with the following persons:
Kenya: M. P. Koinange, Fred Kubai, John Kanina, Naftali Semler, Paulo Mbotela (descendant of freed slaves), Mrs A. Mumwanyi (descendant of freed slaves), Naftali John Simuli (descendant of freed slaves), Immanuel Musula (headmaster of Freretown Primary School), Nancy Mwenja (communicated interview with twelve Kikuyu women who chose to remain anonymous), Mr and Mrs Leonard Beecher, Solomon Joshua, Petro I. Marealle, Joseph Mawalla, and Petro Merinyo.
United Kingdom: Mrs J. W. Arthur, Miss Eleanor Badger, Archdeacon P. G. Bostock.

III *Printed Material*

Printed Missionary Sources

Proceedings of the Church Missionary Society, 1801–.
Extracts of Annual Letters (CMS), 1880–.
Printed Reports (Methodist Missionary Society), 1872–.

Occasional Papers and Pamphlets

Missionary Pamphlets (CMS, London).

Pamphlets on Missions (CMS, London).
Missionary Tracts (CMS, London).
Miscellaneous Papers (CMS, London).
Fugitive Slave Pamphlets (CMS, London).
'Heywood and the first Overseas Missions of the United Methodist Free Church' (cyclostyled copy, 1965, marked N/T 100 in MMS library).
All important cyclostyled-typed manuscripts of CMS, Kikuyu are in Arthur Papers.

Government Publications

a *Kenya*
Annual Reports—Education Department 1925–.
Native Affairs Department 1925–.
Native Labour Commission 1912–1913 (1913).
E. P. C. Girouard, 'Memorandum for Provincial and District Commissioners' (1910).
Report of Education Commission of the East Africa Protectorate (1919).
Report of the Labour Commission (1927).
Kenya Legislative Council Debates: Proceedings become full only after February 17, 1925.

b *United Kingdom*
Correspondence relating to the Masai July, 1911. Cmd. 5585, 1911.
Despatch to the Governor of the East African Protectorate relating to Native Labour and papers connected therewith. Cmd. 873, 1920.
Despatch to the Officer administering the Government of the Kenya Colony and Protectorate relating to Native Labour, Cmd. 1509, 1921.
Papers relating to Native Disturbances in Kenya, March, 1922, Cmd. 1691, 1922.
Indians in Kenya, Cmd. 1922, 1923.
Compulsory Labour for Government Purposes in Kenya, Cmd. 2464, 1925.
Education Policy, in British Tropical Africa, Cmd. 2374, 1925.
Report of the East Africa (Ormsby-Gore) Commission, Cmd. 2387, 1925.
Report of the Hilton Young Commission on Closer Union of the Dependencies in Eastern and Central Africa, Cmd. 3234, 1929.
Memorandum on Native Policy in East Africa, Cmd. 3573, 1929.
Statement of the Conclusions of His Majesty's Government in the

United Kingdom as regards Closer Union in East Africa, Cmd. 3574, 1930.

IV *Periodicals, Journals and Newspapers*

Church Missionary Gleaner (CMS), 1841–1920.
Church Missionary Intelligencer (CMS), 1849–1906 merged into Church Missionary Review (CMS), 1907–1928.
Church Missionary Record (CMS), 1830–1879.
International Review of Missions (pub. International Missionary Council, Edinburgh), 1912.
Kikuyu News (CMS, Kikuyu), 1908–1936.
Taveta Chronicle (CMS, Taveta), 1895–1901.
East Africa Standard, 1905– [formerly, African Standard (Kenya), 1903–1905].
Journal of the [Royal] African Society, 1901–.
Journal of African History, 1960–.
Journal of the [Royal] Anthropological Institute, 1872–.
Round Table, 1910–.

V *Theses*

London University (Senate House Library)

Ajayi, Ade F., *Christian Missions and the Making of Nigeria, 1841–1891.* Ph.D., 1958 (published in London, 1965).
Ayandelle, E. A., *Political and Social Implications of the Missionary Enterprise in the Making of Nigeria, 1842–1914.* Ph.D., 1964 (published in London, 1966).
De Kiewiet, M. J., *History of the Imperial British East Africa Company, 1876–1895.* Ph.D., 1955, unpublished.

Cambridge University

Lonsdale, J. M., *European Penetration into the Nyanza Province of Kenya, 1890–1914.* D.Phil., 1964 (had access to the author's copy). Unpublished.

VI *Contemporaries, Memoirs, Biographies and Others*

Brewin, R. *Memoirs of Mrs Rebecca Wakefield* (London, 1888).
Britton, J., 'Missionary Task in Kenya', *International Review of Missions,* XII, pp. 412–20 (July, 1923).
Bulpett, C. W. L., ed., *John Boyes, King of the Wakikuyu* (London, 1911).

Burton, Richard F., *The Lake Regions of Central Africa*, 2 vols. (London, 1860).

Buxton, M. A., *Kenya Days* (London, 1927).

Crawford, E. M., *By the Equator's Snowy Peak: A Record of Medical Missionary Work and Travel in British East Africa* (London, 1913).

Cust, N., *The Evangelisation of Africa* (London, 1894).

Dawson, E. C., *James Hannington, First Bishop of Eastern Equatorial Africa: A History of his Life and Work, 1847–1885* (London, 1887).

Dawson, E. C., ed., *The Last Journals of Bishop Hannington* (London, 1888).

Deck, L., *Three Years in Savage Africa* (London, 1898).

Eliot, Sir Charles N. E., *The East African Protectorate* (London, 1905).

Fitzgerald, W. W. A., *Travels in the Coastlands of British East Africa, Zanzibar and Pemba* (London, 1898).

Frere, Sir Bartle, *East Africa as a Field for Missionary Labour* (London, 1874).

Guillain, Charles, *Documents sur l'histoire, la géographie et le commerce de l'Afrique orientale*, 3 vols. (Paris, 1856).

Hardinge, A. H., *A Diplomatist in the East* (London, 1928).

Hobley, Charles W., *Kenya from Chartered Company to Crown Colony: Thirty years of exploration and administration in British East Africa* (London, 1929).

——, 'Further researches into Kikuyu and Kamba religious beliefs and customs', *Journal of the Anthropological Institute*, XLI, pp. 406–57, (1911).

Hopkins, A. J., *Trail Blazers and Road Makers* (New York, n.d.).

Hore, E. C., *Tanganyika, Eleven years in Central Africa* (London, 1892).

Hotchkiss, W. R., *Then and Now in Kenya: Forty adventurous years in East Africa* (London, 1937).

Hutchinson, Edward, *The Slave Trade of Africa* (London, 1874).

——, *The Lost Continent, Its Re-discovery and Recovery* (London, 1879).

Jackson, Sir Frederick, *Early Days in East Africa* (London, 1930).

Johnston, H. H., *The Kilimanjaro Expedition* (London, 1886).

Jones, Thomas Jesse, *Education in East Africa* (New York, 1924).

Junod, H. P., 'Bantu Marriage and Christian Society', *Bantu Studies*, xi, pp. 26–29 (1941).

Keller, M., *Twenty Years in Africa* (Toronto, n.d.).

Kirsop, Joseph, *Life of Robert Moss Ormerod; Missionary to East Africa* (London, 1901).

Krapf, J. Ludwig, *Vocabulary of Six East African Languages*

(*Kisuaheli, Kinika, Kikamba, Kipokomo, Kihia, Kigalla*) (Tübingen, 1850).
——, *Travels, Researches and Missionary Labours During an Eighteen Years' Residence in Eastern Africa* (London, 1860).
Livingstone, David, *Missionary Travels and Researches in South Africa: Including a Sketch of Sixteen Years' Residence in the Interior of Africa* (London, 1857).
——, *Narrative of an Expedition to the Zambesi and its Tributaries* (London, 1865).
——, *Last Journals*, 2 vols. (London, 1874).
Lugard, F. D., *The Rise of our East African Empire*, 2 vols. (Edinburgh, 1893).
Maples, Chancey, *Letters and Journals* (London, 1897).
McDermott, P. L., *I.B.E.A.* (London, 1893).
Meinertzhagen, Col., *Kenya Diary, 1902–1906* (Edinburgh, 1957).
New, Charles, *Life, Wanderings and Labours in Eastern Africa* London, 1873).
Norden, Herman, *White and Black in East Africa: Travel and Observation in two African Crown Colonies (Kenya and Uganda)* (London, 1924).
Orde-Brown, G. St. J., *The Vanishing Tribes of Kenya* (London, 1925).
Oldham, Joseph H., and Gipson, B. D., *The Remaking of Man in Africa* (London, 1931).
——, 'Christian civilisation in Africa, as seen at the International Conf. at le Zoute, 1926', *International Review of Missions* (January, 1927).
——, 'Christian missions and African Labour', *International Review of Missions*, X, pp. 183–195 (April, 1921).
Peel, W., 'Among the Wadigo and Wagiriama of British East Africa', *Church Missionary Review*, LXII, i, pp. 163–168 (1911).
Peters, Carl, trns. Dulcken, H. W., *New Light on Dark Africa: being a narrative of the German Emin Pasha expedition* (Munich and Leipzig, 1891).
Philp, H. R. A., *A New Day in Kenya* (London, 1936).
Price, W. S., *My Third Campaign in East Africa* (London, 1890).
Ross, McGregor W., *Kenya from Within* (London, 1927).
Rodd, Rennell, ed., *The British Mission to Uganda in 1893 by Sir G. Portal* (London, 1894).
Smith, H. M., *Frank, Bishop of Zanzibar* (London, 1926).
Smith, E. W., *The Christian Mission in Africa* (London, 1926).
Stock, Eugene, *History of the Church Missionary Society* (3 vols. 1899, iv, 1916) 4 vols. (London, 1899–1916).
Stanley, H. M. *How I Found Livingstone*, 2nd ed. (London, 1872).

——, *Through the Dark Continent*, 2 vols. (London, 1878).

Thomson, Joseph, *Through Masai Land*, 2nd ed. (London, 1885).

Townsend, W. J., Workman, H. B., and Eayrs, George, eds., *A New History of Methodism*, 2 vols. (London, 1909).

Tucker, A. R., *Eighteen Years in Uganda and East Africa* (London, 1908).

Wakefield, E. S., *Thomas Wakefield, Missionary and Geographical Pioneer in East Equatorial Africa* (London, 1904).

Wakefield, T., 'Routes of Native Caravans from the Coast to the Interior of Eastern Africa', *Journal of the Royal Geographical Society*, XL, pp. 303–338 (1870).

Willoughby, W. C., *The Soul of the Bantu* (London, 1928).

Wray, Alfred J., *Kenya, Our Newest Colony, 1882–1912* (London, n.d.).

Ward, Gertrude, ed., *Letters of Bishop Tozer, 1863–1873* (London, 1902).

Weston, Frank, *The Case against Kikuyu: a study in vital principles* (London, 1914).

Willis, J. J., *An African Church in Building* (London, 1925).

Secondary Sources

Achebe, Chinua, *Things Fall Apart* (London, 1958).

'An Experiment in African Education in Kenya', *The Round Table*, XX, pp. 558–572 (June, 1930).

Andersson, Efraim, *Messianic Popular Movements in the Lower Congo* (Uppsala, 1958).

Ajayi, J. F. A., *Christian Missions in Nigeria 1841–1891; The Making of a New Elite* (London, 1965).

Ayendelle, E. A., *The Missionary Impact on Modern Nigeria, 1824–1914* (London, 1966).

Attwater, Donald, *The White Fathers in Africa* (London, 1937).

Axelson, Eric, *South-East Africa, 1488–1530* (Aberdeen, 1940).

Bascom, W. R., 'African Culture and the Missionary', *Civilisations*, III, pp. 491–504 (1953).

Bates, M. Searle, *Data on the Distribution of the Missionary Enterprise* (London, 1943).

Beaver, H. Pierce, *Christianity and African Education* (Grand Rapids, Michigan, 1966).

Beaver, Harold, *The Confessions of Jotham Simiyu* (London, 1965).

Bennett, G., 'Imperial Paternalism', in Robinson, K., and Madden, F., eds., *Essays in Imperial Government presented to Margery Perham* (London, 1963).

——, *Kenya, A Political History: The Colonial Period* (London, 1963).

Bennett, N. R., 'The British on Kilimanjaro, 1884–1892', *Tanganyika*

Notes and Records, No. 63, pp. 229–244 (September, 1964).

Bernardi, Bernado, *The Mugwe, A Failing Prophet* (London, 1959).

Bewes, T. F. C., 'Work of the Christian Church among the Kikuyu', *International Affairs*, XXIX, pp. 316–25 (July, 1953).

Blixen, Karen, *Out of Africa* (New York, 1952).

Boxer, C. R., and Azevede, De Carlos, *Fort Jesus and the Portuguese in Mombasa, 1593–1729* (London, 1960).

Buell, R. L., *The Native Problem in Africa*, 2 vols. (New York, 1928).

Cagnolo, C., *The Akikuyu—their customs, traditions and folklore* (Nyen Catholic Mission, 1933).

Capen, M. G., *Towards Unity in Kenya* (Nairobi, 1962).

Carothers, J. C., *The Psychology of Mau Mau* (Nairobi, 1954).

Corfield, F. D., *The Origins and Growth of Mau Mau* (Nairobi, 1960).

Coupland, Reginald, *East Africa and Its Invaders, from the Earliest Times to the death of Seyyid Said in 1856* (Oxford, 1938).

——, *The Exploitation of East Africa 1856–1890: The Slave Trade and the Scramble* (London, 1939).

Dougall, J. W. C., 'The Case for and against Mission Schools', *Journal of the African Society*, XXXVIII (1939).

——, 'Education and Evangelism', *International Review of Missions*, XXXVI, pp. 313–23 (July, 1947).

——, *Christianity and the Sex Education of the African* (London, 1937).

——, *Christians in the African Revolution* (Edinburgh, 1963).

Delarignette, Robert L., *Christianisme et Colonialisme* (Paris, 1960).

Dundas, Charles, *Kilimanjaro and Its People* (London, 1924).

Dilley, M. R., *British Policy in Kenya Colony* (New York, 1937).

Frank, William, *Habari na desturi za Waribe* (London, 1953).

Freyre, G., *The Masters and the Slaves* (Trans. Samuel Pitman) (New York, 1964).

Gale, H. P., *Uganda and the Mill Hill Fathers* (London, 1959).

Gatheru, Mugo, *Child of Two Worlds* (London, 1964).

Gregory, Robert G., *Sidney Webb and East Africa; Labour's Experiment with the Doctrine of Native Paramountcy* (Berkeley and Los Angeles, 1962).

Groves, Charles Pelham, *The Planting of Christianity in Africa*, 4 vols. (London, 1948–58).

Hanna, A. J., *The Beginnings of Nyasaland and North-Eastern Rhodesia 1859–1895* (Oxford, 1956).

Hall, D., 'The Native Question in Kenya', *The Nineteenth Century and After*, cvii, pp. 70–80 (1930).

Hailey, Lord, *An African Survey* (London, 1938; and revised, London, 1958).

Harris, Lyndon, 'Missionary on the East African Coast', *International Review of Missions*, XXXV, pp. 183-6 (April, 1946).

Harlow, Vincent, Chilver, E. M., and Smith, Alison, eds., *History of East Africa*, II (Oxford, 1965).

Herskovits, Melville J., *The Human Factor in Changing Africa* (London, 1962).

Hetherwick, Alexander, *The Gospel and the African* (Edinburgh, 1932).

Hodgkin, Thomas, *Nationalism in Colonial Africa* (London, 1956).

Hollingsworth, L. W., *Zanzibar under the Foreign Office 1890-1913* (London, 1953).

Kayamba, H. M. T., 'The Modern Life of the East African Native', *Africa*, V, pp. 50-59 (January, 1932).

Kenyatta, Jomo, 'Kikuyu religion, ancestor-worship and sacrificial practices', *Africa*, X, No. 3 (July, 1937).

——, *Facing Mount Kenya* (London, 1938).

Kilson, Martin L., Jr., 'Land and the Kikuyu : A study of the relationship between land and Kikuyu political movements', *Journal of Negro History*, XL, pp. 103-53 (April, 1955).

Kittler, Glen D., *The White Fathers* (New York, 1957).

Klaus, J. F., 'The Early Missions of the Swan River District, 1821-1869', *Saskatchewan History*, xvii, No. 2, pp. 61-76 (Spring, 1964).

Koinange, P. M., *The People of Kenya Speak for Themselves* (Detroit, 1955).

Kuper, Hilda, 'The Swazi Reaction to Missions', *African Studies*, v, pp. 176-188 (1946).

Lambert, H. E., *Kikuyu Social and Political Institutions* (London, 1956).

Latourette, K. S., *A History of the Expansion of Christianity*, 7 vols. (London, 1945-47).

Leakey, L. S. B., 'The Kikuyu Problem of Initiation of Girls', *Journal of the Royal Anthropological Institute*, lxi, pp. 277-85 (1931).

——, *Kenya: Contrasts and Problems* (London, 1935).

——, *Defeating Mau Mau* (London, 1954).

——, *Mau Mau and the Kikuyu* (London, 1952).

Leys, Norman, *Kenya* (London, 1924).

Low, D. A., 'Religion and Society in Buganda, 1875-1900', *East African Studies*, No. 8 (Kampala, 1957).

Lindblom, G., *The Akamba in British East Africa*, 2nd ed. (Uppsala, 1920).

Mannoni, O. (Trans. Pamela Powesland), *Prospero and Caliban, The Psychology of Colonisation* (New York, 1956).

Maxwell, G. V. (Chairman), *Native land tenure in Kikuyu Province:*

Report of Committee, November, 1929 (Nairobi, 1930).

Mockerie, P. G., An African Speaks for his People (London, 1934).

Morris, William Dale, The Christian Origins of Social Revolt (London, 1949).

Ngala, R. G., Nchi na desturi za Wagiriama (Dar-es-Salaam, 1956).

Ngugi, James, The River Between (London, 1965).

Oliver, Roland, The Missionary Factor in East Africa (London, 1952).

——, How Christian is Africa? (London, 1956).

——, and Mathew, Gervase, eds., History of East Africa, Vol. I (Oxford, 1963).

Parrinder, Geoffrey, Religion in an African City (London, 1953).

Perham, Margery, ed., The Diaries of Lord Lugard, 4 vols. (London, 1959).

Porter, A. T., Creoldom: A Study of the Development of Freetown Society (Oxford, 1963).

Prins, A. H. J., The Coastal Tribes of the North Eastern Bantu (London, 1952).

Ranger, Terence, 'African Attempts to Control Education in East and Central Africa, 1900–1939', Past and Present (December, 1965).

Richards, C. G., Archdeacon Owen of Kavirondo (Nairobi, 1947).

Robinson, R. E., Callagher, J., and Denny, A., Africa and the Victorians: The Official Mind of Imperialism (London, 1961).

Ross, Emery, 'Christianity in Africa', Annals of the American Academy of Political and Social Sciences, ccxcviii, pp. 161–169 (1955).

Rotberg, I. R., Christian Missionaries and the Creation of Northern Rhodesia (Princeton, 1965).

Savage, Donald and J. F. Munro, 'Carrier Corps Recruitment in the British East Africa Protectorate, 1914–1918', Journal of African History, VII, No. 2, pp. 313–342 (1966).

Seaver, George, David Livingstone: His Life and Letters (New York, 1957).

Shepperson, George, 'The Politics of African Church Separatist Movements in British Central Africa, 1892–1916', Africa, XXIV, pp. 233-246 (1954).

——, and Thomas Price, Independent African: John Chilembwe and the Origins, Setting and Significance of the Nyasaland Native Rising of 1915 (Edinburgh, 1958).

Slade, Ruth, English-Speaking Missions in the Congo, 1878–1908 (Brussels, 1959).

Stuart-Watt, E., Africa's Dome of Mystery ... History of the Wachagga people of Kilimanjaro (London, 1930).

Strandes, J., Die Portugiesenzeit von Deutsch- und Englishsch-

Ostafrika (Berlin, 1899). English translation, Wall, J. F., trans., Kirkman, J. S., ed., 'The Portuguese in East Africa', *Transactions of Kenya Historical Society*, II (Nairobi, 1961).

Sundkler, B. G. M., *Bantu Prophets in South Africa* (London, 1948).

Taylor, J. V., *The Growth of the Church in Buganda* (London, 1958).

——, and Lehmann, Dorethea A., *Christians of the Copperbelt: The Growth of the Church in Northern Rhodesia* (London, 1961).

Thonnen, J. P., *Black Martyrs* (London, 1942).

Townsend, Mary E., *The Rise and Fall of Germany's Colonial Empire* (London, 1930).

Trimingham, J. Spencer, *Islam in East Africa* (Oxford, 1964).

Warren, Max, *The Missionary Movement from Britain in Modern History* (London, 1965).

Webster, J. B., *The African Churches among the Yoruba 1888–1892* (London, 1964).

Welbourn, F. B., *East African Rebels* (London, 1961).

——, and Ogot, B. A., *A Place to Feel at Home: A Study of Two Independent Churches in Western Kenya* (London, 1961).

Westermann, Diedrich, *Africa and Christianity* (London, 1937).

Wilson, Monica Hunter, *Communal Rituals of the Nyakyusa* (London, 1959).

Index

Abolition of slavery, 52, 53, 54, 55, 58, 60
African Workers' Council, 85, 88
Akamba, 36, 38, 43, 71, 73, 107
Anglo-German Treaty, 45, 47, 52
Anti-Slavery Society, 52, 53, 55, 57
Arab attacks, 21, 52
Arthur, John W., 109, 118, 119, 121, 123, 124, 125, 126, 131, 134, 136, 147, 158

Barlow, Ruffel, 120, 129
Binns, H., 21, 22, 32, 34, 36, 72, 85, 110, 111
Bishops Memorandum, 122, 124
Blantyre Mission, 16, 17
Bombay Africans, 13, 18, 63, 66, 68, 71, 72, 74, 75, 77, 78, 79, 80, 83
British Foreign Office, 55, 58, 59
British Protestant missions, 2, 20
Buganda, 24, 47, 91
Burt, Rev. F., 86, 87
Byles, Captain Mather, 17, 18, 19

Chagga, 32, 33, 34, 43, 51, 155
  hostility towards CMS, 47
  schools, 142, 145
Chingulia, Don Jerome, 6, 7
Church Missionary Intelligencer, The, 39, 76

Church Missionary Society (CMS), 5, 7, 8, 11, 12, 14, 20, 26, 29, 32, 94, 120, 131
  at Blantyre, 17
  expelled from German East Africa, 48
  and ex-slaves, 64
  at Freretown, 15, 46
  and Hardinge, 59
  in Highlands, 140
  intermediary between Germans and Meli, 50, 51
  and Mandara, 39
  missionaries in Zanzibar, 34
  at Mombasa, 45
  and Nyika, 71
  schools, 142, 143, 146, 147, 154, 162
  in Sierra Leone, 11, 12, 63
  and slavery, 52
Crowther, Samuel, 12, 74, 75, 79, 80

Dagoretti, 129, 130
David, George, 32, 65, 68, 69, 74, 75, 76, 80, 81, 85
Deimler, James, 85, 86, 87, 88
Dougall, J.W.C., 149, 150

East African Protectorate, 46, 51, 56

Eliot, Charles, N.E., 93, 98, 125

Fitch, E.A., 34, 40, 47
Forster, W.E., 20
Freed slave settlements, 11-29
Freretown, 8, 12, 15, 16, 20, 24,
  25, 34, 36, 46, 63, 66, 72, 76,
  80, 84, 143, 144
Fulladoyo, 24, 28

Galla, 5, 32, 33, 37, 39, 43, 97
German East Africa, 26, 117
German East Africa Company,
  47, 48

Handford, J.W., 16, 32, 75, 77,
  83, 142
Hannington, James, 34, 35, 38, 73,
  84, 85, 106
Hardinge, Arthur, 44, 45, 46, 51,
  54, 55, 56, 58, 59, 60
Hobley, Charles, 60, 119
Holmwood, Frederick, 17, 18, 19,
  25, 81
Hooper, Handley, 131, 148, 149,
  156, 161

Imperial British East Africa
  Company (IBEAC), 25, 27, 28,
  29, 44, 46, 59

Jackson, Frederick, 27, 101
Jeanes school, 150, 151
Jilore, 70, 72, 98, 142
Jomvu, 24, 25, 36
Jones, William, 14, 15, 28, 32, 35,
  68, 69, 70, 71, 72, 73, 74, 76,, 81,
  82, 83, 86, 89

Kavirondo, 152, 153
Kenya, 1, 2, 5, 6, 7, 8, 9, 10, 13,
  32, 35, 51, 100, 101, 118, 121
Kenyatta, Jomo, 136, 145, 163
Kikuyu Central Association, 9
Kilimanjaro, 8, 32, 34, 39, 48
Kimberley, Lord, 54, 55
Kimweri, 8, 33

Kirk, Sir John, 17, 20, 21, 25, 79
Krapf, Johann Ludwig, 5, 7, 8, 33

Lamb, J.A., 13, 32, 68, 74, 75, 77
Lamu, 6, 44, 57
Leakey, Rev. Harry, 110, 131, 133,
  135, 148
Livingstone, 60, 65, 141

Mackenzie, Donald, 56
Mackenzie, W., 27, 28, 29
MacKinnon, William, 25, 95
Malinda, 6, 44, 57
Mandara, 8, 32, 34, 37, 38, 39, 40,
  47, 48,
Marealle, 48, 49
Masai, 35, 36, 37, 39, 43, 70, 73,
  98, 128
Masailand, 35
Mathews, General Lloyd, 29, 34,
  51
Mau mau war, 2, 10, 126, 164
Mazrui families, 43-44
Meli, 48, 49, 51
Menzies, A., 16, 17, 18, 75, 76, 77,
  78, 80-81
Mombasa, 5, 6, 12, 13, 15, 19, 21,
  24, 25, 26, 43, 44, 46, 57, 105,
  109, 148
Moshi, 32, 34, 38, 47, 50, 71

New, Charles, 32, 33
Northey, Governor, 118, 122, 125
Nyika (Mijikenda people), 5, 32,
  33, 35, 36, 37, 40, 43, 65, 69, 71,
  72, 105, 145

Oldham, J.H., 127, 154
Oliver, Professor Roland, 1, 24,
  141
Ormeroid, Robert Moss, 33, 93

Parker, Bishop Henry, 40, 106,
  141, 142
Peel, William George, 60, 78, 86,
  87, 91, 95
Peters, Carl, 48, 49
Philp, Horace, 121, 122, 149

183

Pokomo, 32, 43, 93, 101, 107
Price, William Salt, 12, 13, 26, 28,
    64, 66, 75, 77, 82, 141, 144

Rabai Mpia, 5, 7, 15, 23, 24, 25,
    28, 34, 36, 41, 52, 59, 66, 69,
    71, 72, 105
Rebmann, Johannes, 5, 7, 8, 65
Ribe, 24, 28, 32, 141
Ross, McGregor, 127, 131
Russell, Commander, W., 16, 34

Salisbury, Lord, 25, 56, 60
Scott, Henry, 95, 97, 100, 105
Seimler, Ishmael, 74, 76, 85, 86
Sharanpur, 12, 64
Shimba Hill, 70, 72
Sierra Leone, 11, 63, 83
Slave uprising, 22, 23
Smith, Euan, 28, 54
Smith, Thomas, 76, 77
Somali, 37, 43
Steggal, Albert, 47, 50
Streeter, J.R., 16, 17, 18, 22, 75,
    77, 81
Swahili-Arabs, 8, 19, 26, 27, 36

Taita, 70, 142
Takaungu, 44, 51, 52, 72
Tanganyika, 24, 25, 33, 35, 71
Taylor, W.E., 45, 142
Teita, 38, 40, 41

Thuku, H., 123, 129, 130, 132, 133,
    135, 136, 149
Tucker, Alfred, 46, 47, 58, 60, 85,
    91

Uganda, 35, 38, 43, 51, 91, 106
Ukambani, 8, 34, 38
United Free Methodists, 7, 101,
    140, 141
United Methodist Free Church
    (UMFC) 25, 32, 33, 92, 94
Usambara, 32, 33

Vanga, 44, 58
Ven, Henry, 12, 141

Wakefield, Thomas, 32, 33, 37,
    38, 141
Wali of Mombasa, 22, 25, 51, 59
Wanjika, 33, 72
Willis, J.J., 92, 104, 122
Wray, J.A., 34, 35, 40, 41, 70
Wright, Henry, 76, 106

Young Kikuyu Association, 129,
    130, 131, 132, 133, 134, 135,
    136

Zanzibar, 7, 25, 28, 35, 45, 51, 52,
    53, 56, 66, 83
    Sultan of, 33, 35, 39, 43, 45,
    84, 106

184